Anne Rowena's

HANDKNITTING COLLECTION

Anne Rowena's
HANDKNITTING COLLECTION

photography by Martin Palmer

A DAVID & CHARLES CRAFT BOOK

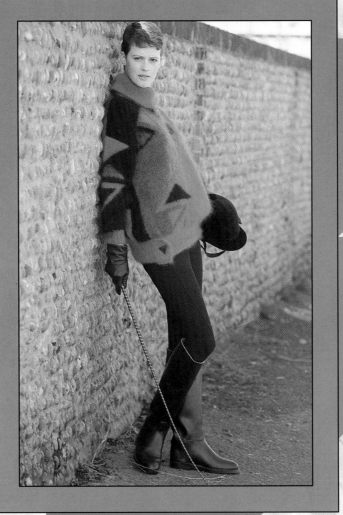

British Library Cataloguing in Publication Data
Rowena, Anne
    Anne Rowena's handknitting collection.
    1. Knitting. British designs
    I. Title
    746.43′2

    ISBN 0-7153-9428-2

Phototypeset by ABM Typographics Limited, Hull
and printed in West Germany
by Mohndruck Gmbh
for David & Charles Publishers plc
Brunel House   Newton Abbot   Devon

Distributed in the United States by
Sterling Publishing Co Inc,
387 Park Avenue South, New York, NY 10016–8810

CONTENTS

INTRODUCTION

ABOUT ME

I am a self-taught knitter and designer, having learnt to knit as a child, dismissed the hobby for many years while school studies took over, then later, when already starting out in work, taking it up again. For a few years I worked as a secretary and an air stewardess, but dissatisfaction with work led me to start my own business selling knitwear designs as made-up jumpers. Initially I sold to just a few shops in London, but soon was exporting to the USA and Canada and the business has grown from there. I launched a range of knitting kits which now sell through knitting shops throughout the UK and through magazine offers, making my designs more accessible to the home market at a much reduced price. My shop in Cambridge was opened in 1985 selling my own jumpers along with a good selection from other designers. The shop soon expanded into a yarn store too, with an emphasis on natural yarns with a fashion image. I have my own range of mohair and now most of my designs can be bought either already made up or as patterns with the yarn, which has led to this book being produced.

ABOUT THE BOOK

This book is a collection of favourite designs I have done over the last few years. They fall into two main groups. Firstly, mohair, which is my favourite yarn to work with – bright, bold designs and generally quick to knit. Secondly, wool, in the forms of double knitting, chunky and 4 ply. These are more subtle designs although some are very intricate and should be tackled only by more experienced knitters. Most of the designs are for women but I have included three for men too. Both beginners and experienced knitters can enjoy this book, but I do not attempt to teach how to knit. You should be able to cast on, knit, purl and cast off; if you cannot, there are plenty of books available to help, but the best way to learn is to ask someone to teach you personally. A few techniques are explained in this introduction to help in the general working of patterns, and where more detailed help is required knitting tips are included with the relevant pattern. Each pattern is graded 'easy', 'needs some experience' or 'difficult', to give a guide as to which ones to attempt. Perhaps start with an easy one and work your way up.

ABOUT THE DESIGNS

As you will soon notice by looking through the book, my sweaters are very basic shapes – mainly square, dropped shoulders with a simple neckline. They are intended as timeless pieces of clothing and as such do not follow any particular fashion trend of the moment. My influences have been mainly geometric shapes, floral displays, fabric designs and fashion themes. The use of colour is extremely important. Bright shades are always popular, the more muted ones seem to suit almost everyone. Using this principle, I hope many of you will attempt to work out your own designs; use the plain patterns as a guide for stitches and measurements then draw out a graph with the correct number of stitches and rows for your size and transfer your design onto the graph paper. Once you have worked out your colours and drawn them in, you're ready to start. Don't make it too difficult to begin with and you'll soon be walking around in your very own 'original handknit'.

ABOUT THE YARNS

The yarns used throughout the book are standard yarns for their type, ie the double knitting patterns can be used with any good-quality double knitting as most knit up to the same tension these days. I have stated the specific yarns used in each case, but don't worry if you can't get them where you live. Either choose an alternative yarn or send for details of our mail-order price list as all the designs are available as kits (see below). When substituting yarn the most important thing to remember is to match the tension. Nowadays the ballband gives lots of information, ie needles to use, tension square and even the length of yarn to each ball. Using this information you can easily substitute different yarns.

ABOUT THE KITS

All the designs are available as knitting kits direct from my shop in Cambridge. The kits include sufficient yarn to make up the largest size, buttons where applicable and an Anne Rowena label. Please send for an up-to-date price list from Anne Rowena, 4 Trinity Street, Cambridge, CB2 1SU or ring (0223) 66841.

ABOUT THE PATTERNS

Generally each pattern is written in three sizes, the larger sizes in brackets. If only one figure is stated, all sizes apply. Measurements are given in centimetres and inches and a shape guide is included with each pattern to help you obtain the correct size. Please read all the Knitting Notes below before beginning any of the patterns as most are relevant to each pattern.

KNITTING NOTES

CHARTS

Unless otherwise stated, read the charts row by row starting at the bottom right. Read odd-numbered rows from right to left – knit rows, and even-numbered rows from left to right – purl rows (stocking stitch). A few patterns have exceptions to this rule when working a 'mirror' image, but this is dealt with in the patterns themselves. In most cases do not work to the end of the chart as this may not be your size, keep measuring the work until you obtain the correct length. You should not need to knit more than the length of the chart if your tension is correct, but if you choose to work to a longer length follow the pattern on its natural course or, if the pattern stops naturally, work the extra length plain. Some people have trouble with highly detailed charts on a small grid. It does help to have the charts enlarged on a photocopier, or to colour sections in first to help differentiate between pattern detail.

Casting On and Casting Off

Casting on and casting off are the first steps to ensure a good finish to the final garment. If your casting on and casting off are too tight, ie do not stretch with the main part of the rib or jumper, try using larger needles for casting on and casting off only. If they are too loose, ie loopy stitches on the cast on and cast off rows, use smaller needles. However, do not tighten the casting off too much otherwise the sleeve tops will not fit into the required space and the neck may be too tight to go over your head. Knitting elastic can be used in ribs to help keep their shape, either while working the ribs, or added later.

FINISHING TOUCHES

Seams   I recommend backstitch on shoulder and sleeve-top seams as this is neat and hides the cast-off edges. All other seams and ribs can be joined with edge-to-edge seams for less bulk and to make the work lie flat.

Ends   Knit or weave the ends in where possible as you go along, to save having to darn them in at the end. Where this is not possible, leave a length of 5cm [2in] and darn in with a needle before sewing up. *Never* knot and cut – the knot will soon

wear undone, the yarn will pull loose and a hole will appear.

Pressing   Always note first whether pressing is recommended on the ballband. Most jumpers benefit from a light pressing before sewing up and the seams after sewing up, using a mid to hot iron over a damp cloth. However, be wary of ribs and cable patterns, if these are pressed they lose all their stretch and texture, so do be careful.

Washing   Unless stated on the ballband, hand wash your handknitted items in warm or cold water using a reputable brand of washing powder or liquid. A short spin or rolling up in a towel will remove the bulk of the water. Leave the garment to lie flat and dry in its own time, easing it into its correct shape while drying.

TENSION

This is very important. It refers to the tightness or slackness of a piece of knitted work. I have quoted a tension over a 10cm [4in] square, so to work out your tension knit up a square using the recommended size needles. Pin the square out flat and, using a ruler, count the stitches and rows. If you have more than recommended, your knitting is tight and you need to use a size or two larger needle. If you have less than stated, your knitting is loose and needs a size or two smaller needle. Do the square again on the different sized needles and measure again. Repeat the process until you get it right.

Points to remember about tension

* No two knitters are ever alike so don't despair if you are close in stitches but not in rows, or vice versa. Generally choose a looser tension rather than tighter, as this will result in a slightly bigger jumper rather than too small. You can always follow the instructions for the smaller size to allow for the difference.
* The number of stitches is more important than the number of rows as the width cannot be adjusted once the work has started, the length can.
* Always re-do a tension square when using a different yarn – never assume your tension will work out the same as with the suggested type.

* Make sure your casting on and casting off rows are neither too tight nor too loose (see Casting On and Casting Off below).

WORKING WITH MANY COLOURS

Most of the designs in this book are worked with more than one or two colours. With a little preparation this can be managed without the frustration of tangled balls of yarn.

* Firstly, cut and join the colours as you need them rather than take the yarn across large areas at the back of the work, which always results in unnecessary loops and pulls the work out of shape.

* For small sections of colour use a length of yarn rather than the whole ball. This is much easier to pull through than a whole ball when yarns get tangled.

* When changing colours mid-row, twist the two colours round each other at the back of work to prevent a hole appearing.

* If you are doing a section of main colour with a small panel of contrast colour of say 2 or 3 stitches, join the contrast colour but loop the main colour across at the back and continue with the row. Any more than 3 stitches and the best result is obtained by joining in a new ball of main colour, again to prevent unnecessary loops and tightening of work.

NEEDLE SIZES

Metric (mm)	Former British	USA
10	000	
9	00	15
8	0	13
7½	1	11
7	2	10½
6½	3	10
6	4	9
5½	5	8
5	6	7
4½	7	6
4	8	5
3¾	9	4
3¼	10	3
3	11	2
2¾	12	1
2¼	13	0
2	14	00

EQUIVALENT TERMS

UK	USA
Cast off	Bind off
Stocking stitch	Stockinette stitch
Tension	Gauge
4 ply	Sport/Lightweight
Double Knitting (DK)	Knitting worsted
Aran/Sport	Fisherman/Medium weight
Chunky	Bulky

ABBREVIATIONS

A-N	contrast colours	**k**	knit
p	purl	**st(s)**	stitch(es)
st st	stocking stitch	**beg**	begin(ning)
g st	garter stitch	**cont**	continue(ing)
tog	together	**foll**	follow(ing)
alt	alternate	**inc**	increase(ing)
rep	repeat(s)(ing)	**rem**	remain(ing)
dec	decrease(ing)	**sl**	slip
patts	pattern(s)	**cm**	centimetre(s)
yrn	yarn	**ws**	wrong side of work
in	inch(es)	**fwd**	forward
rs	right side of work	**pup**	pick up and purl
puk	pick up and knit	**skpo**	slip 1, knit 1, pass slip stitch over
psso	pass slip stitch over		

c2b cable 2 back: slip next stitch onto cable needle and hold at back of work. Knit next stitch, knit stitch from cable needle.

c2f cable 2 front: slip next stitch onto cable needle and hold at front of work. Knit next stitch, knit stitch from cable needle.

c3f cable 3 front: slip next stitch onto cable needle and hold at front of work. Knit next 2 stitches, knit stitch from cable needle.

Special abbreviations relating to only one particular design are explained in that pattern's instructions.

MOHAIR

Mohair comes from the Angora goat – a delicate creature that needs constant and expert attention as it cannot stand extreme climates. Its beautiful long silky wool is extremely strong and durable and retains its magnificent lustre over many years of enjoyment; it is a natural miracle. The word 'mohair' derives from the ancient Arabic word *mukhaya* meaning 'cloth of bright goats' hair'.

These beautiful Angora goats photographed in their natural habitat show the gentle quality which has made them so endearing.

SPOTLIGHT

**Needs some experience

SIZE
To fit bust 87-92(92-98,98-104)cm [34-36(36-38,38-40)in]

MATERIALS
Yarn used in sample
Anne Rowena Mohair
Quantities
Main colour (black) 12 x 25g balls (A)
1st contrast (grey) 8 x 25g balls (B)
2nd contrast (gold) 2 x 25g balls (C)
Alternative yarn
Any mohair that knits up to same tension
Needles
1 pair each 4½mm (7) and 5½mm (5) needles
Buttons
2 x 37mm [1½in] domes

TENSION
Using 5½mm (5) needles over stocking stitch, 14 sts x 18/20 rows = 10 x 10cm [4 x 4in]. (see Tension, page 11).

TIP
The back and front are mirror images of each other. Knit back first then, whilst working front reading the chart in opposite direction, lay the back down, wrong side up, so that you can see more clearly what front should look like as you knit it.

BACK
Rib With 4½mm needles and A, cast on 70(76,82) sts and work k1, p1 rib for 5cm [2in], ending with ws row.
Buttonhole Rib 6, cast off 3 sts, rib to end of row. Next row: rib to cast-off sts, cast on 3 sts, rib 6. Cont to rib until work measures 10cm [4in].
Front flap Cast off first 14 sts and rib to end of row.
Inc row Small: (inc in next st) twice; (rib 1, inc in next st) 26 times; (inc in next st) twice [86 sts]. Medium & Large: rib 1(4); (rib 1, inc in next st) 30 times; rib to end [92(98) sts]. Change to 5½mm needles.
Now foll chart for back working in st st, noting beg and end sts for each

size. Use separate balls of yrn for each block of colour to avoid drawing yrn across at back. Twist yrn round at back to prevent holes appearing. Work until back measures 62(65,68)cm [24½(25½,26¾)in] from beg.
Shoulder shaping Cast off 8(9,10) sts at beg of next 2 rows, cast off 9(10,11) sts at beg of foll 4 rows. Leave rem 34 sts on st holder/spare yrn.

FRONT
Rib With 4½mm needles and A, cast on 56(62,68) sts and work k1, p1 rib for 10cm [4in].
Inc row As for back. Change to 5½mm needles. Foll chart for front until work measures 55(58,61)cm [21½(22¾,24)in] from beg.
Neck shaping Patt first 33(36,39) sts, turn and dec 1 st at beg of next row and every foll alt row to 26(29,32) sts; cont straight until front measures 62(65,68)cm [24½(25½,26¾)in] from beg.

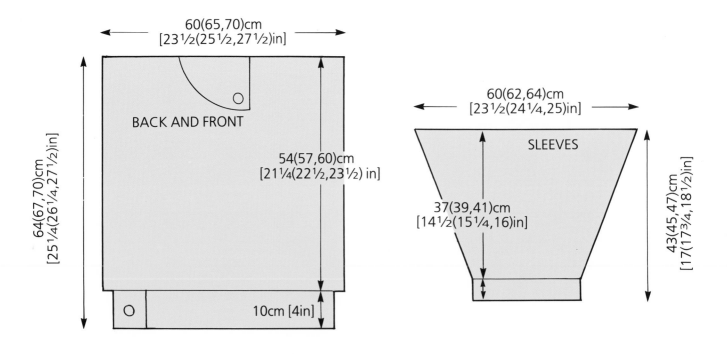

BACK AND FRONT

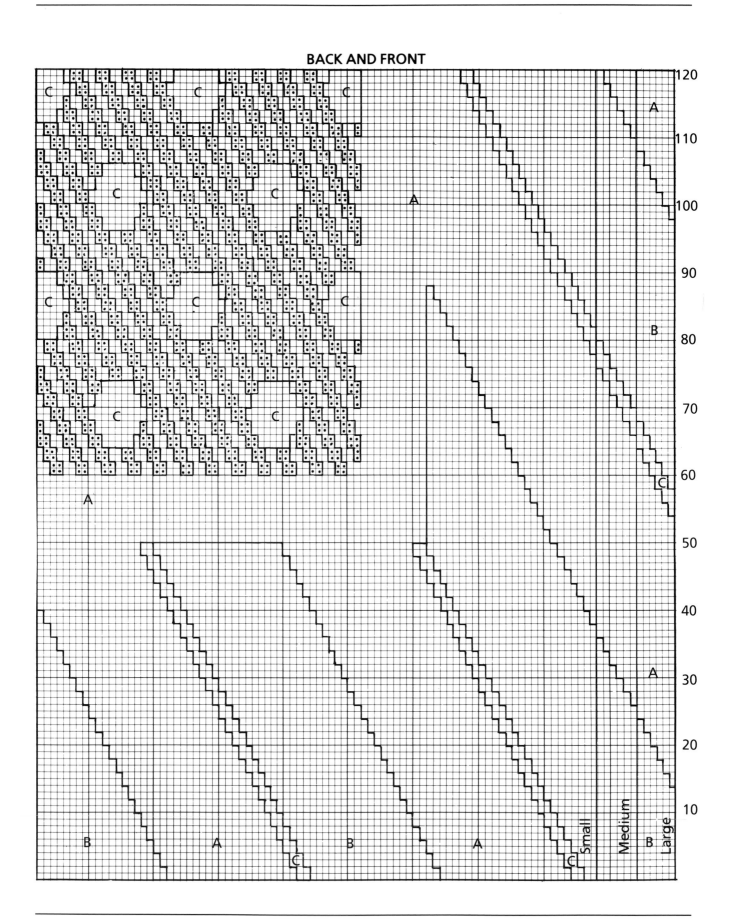

LEFT SLEEVE

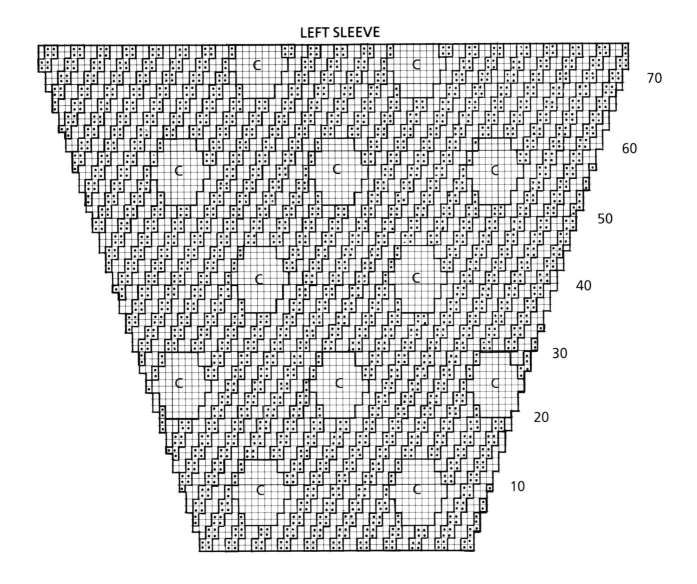

70

60

50

40

30

20

10

KEY

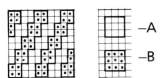

—A

—B

Watch tension on this sleeve
Because of carrying yrn across at
back, you may find work becomes
tight. Try to leave loops loose and use
bigger needles if necessary. Do not
take yrn across back of 'spots' — join
new yrn.

Read Back and Front charts thus

BACK   K rows right to left
          P rows left to right

FRONT (Mirror image)
          K rows left to right
          P rows right to left

RIGHT SLEEVE

Shoulder shaping Cast off 8(9,10) sts at beg of next row, work 1 row. Cast off 9(10,11) sts at beg of next and foll alt row. Thread centre 20 sts onto st holder and work rem 33(36,39) sts to match left side, reversing shapings.

SLEEVES
Rib With 4½mm needles and A, cast on 30 sts and work k1, p1 rib for 6cm [2½in].
Inc row Rib 3; (inc in next st, rib 1) 12 times; rib to end [42 sts]. Change to 5½mm needles and foll charts given for sleeves.

Shaping Inc 1 st each end of 4th and every foll 3rd row (4th, 7th, 10th etc) to end. When sleeve measures 43(45,47)cm [17(17¾,18½)in] from beg, cast off loosely.

COLLAR
Join right shoulder, using backstitch so that no cast-off sts are visible. With rs facing and using 4½mm needles and A, puk 14 sts down left side, 20 sts across front, 14 sts up right side and 34 sts from back [82 sts]. Work k1, p1 rib for 17cm [6¾in] ending with front, rs of jumper, facing.
Buttonhole Rib 6, cast off 3 sts, rib

to end. Next row: rib 73, cast on 3 sts, rib 6. Cont to rib normally until collar measures 20cm [8in]. Cast off ribwise.

FINISHING OFF
Join left shoulder using backstitch. Cont to sew 5cm [2in] of collar ensuring that collar seam is on inside when collar folds over shoulder. Sew in sleeves, using backstitch, matching centre of each sleeve top with shoulder seam. Sew side and sleeve seams. Seams may be pressed using hot iron and damp cloth, but do not press ribs. Sew on buttons to correspond with buttonholes.

FLOWER TRELLIS

SIZE
To fit bust 87-92(92-98,98-104)cm [34-36(36-38,38-40)in]

MATERIALS
Yarn used in sample
Anne Rowena Mohair
Quantities
Main colour (grey) 10 x 25g balls (A)
1st contrast (royal) 6 x 25g balls (B)
2nd contrast (black) 3 x 25g balls (C)
3rd contrast (fuchsia) 2 x 25g balls (D)
4th contrast (purple) 1 x 25g ball (E)
Alternative yarn
Any mohair that knits up to same tension
Needles
1 pair each 4½mm (7) and 5½mm (5) needles
Buttons
2 x 37mm [1½in] domes

TENSION
Using 5½mm (5) needles over stocking stitch, 14 sts x 18/20 rows = 10 x 10cm [4 x 4in] (see Tension, page 11).

BACK
Rib With 4½mm needles and A, cast on 56(62,68) sts and work k1, p1 rib for 10cm [4in].
Inc row Small: (inc in next st) twice; (rib 1, inc in next st) 26 times; (inc in next st) twice [86 sts]. Medium & Large: rib 1(4); (rib 1, inc in next st) 30 times, rib to end [92(98) sts].
Change to 5½mm needles.
Work in stripe patt as follows:
Row 1: (rs) with B, k.
Row 2: with B, p.
Rows 3-8: rep rows 1 & 2 three times.
Row 9: with C, k.
Row 10: with C, p.
These 10 rows form the stripe patt.
Rep them once more. Now beg working in patt from chart as folls:
Patt row 1: k53(56,59)A, 3C, 30(33,34)B, 0(0,2)C.
Patt row 2: p0(0,3)C, 31(34,34)B, 3C, 52(55,58)A.
Cont in st st throughout, complete the 60 rows of patt as shown in chart **. Cut off C and rejoin it at beg of row. Beg row 9, work in stripe patt until back measures 67(70,73)cm [26½(27½,28¾)in] from beg,
ending with ws row.
Shoulder shaping Cast off 11(12,13) sts at beg of next 6 rows. Cut off yrn and leave rem sts on a st holder/spare yrn.

FRONT
Work as for back to **.
Divide for neck opening With C, k33(36,39), turn, leave rem sts on a spare needle. Work on first set of sts as folls:
*****Next row** With C, p. Now, beg row 1, cont working in stripe patt until front measures same as back to beg of shoulder shaping, ending at side edge.
Shoulder shaping Cast off 11(12,13) sts at beg of next and foll alt row. Work 1 row. Cast off***.
Return to sts on spare needle. With rs facing, sl first 20 sts onto a holder for neck inset and collar, join in C to next st and k to end of row. Work as given for first side from *** to ***

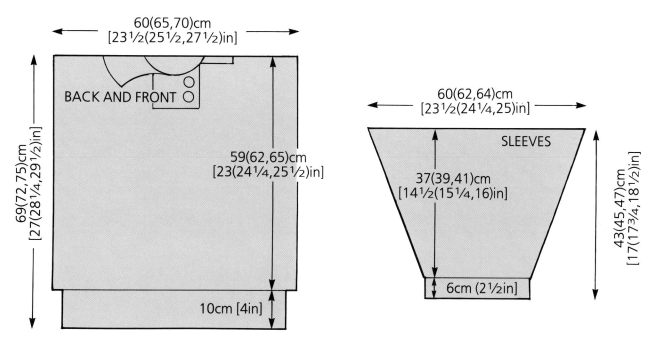

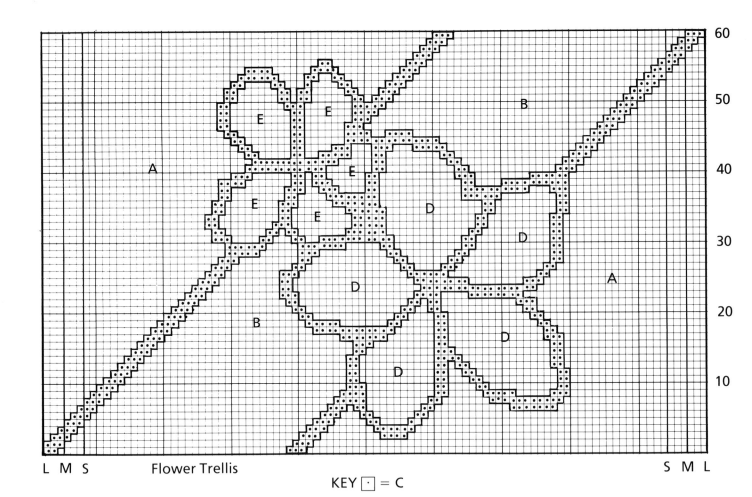

L M S   Flower Trellis   S M L

KEY ⬚ = C

SLEEVES

Rib With 4½mm needles and A, cast on 30 sts and work k1, p1 rib for 6cm [2½in].

Inc row Rib 3; (inc in next st, rib 1) 12 times; rib to end [42 sts]. Change to 5½mm needles.

Beg row 1, work 30 rows in stripe patt as given for back, but at same time inc 1 st each end of 4th and every foll 3rd row [60 sts]. Cut off B and C. Still inc on every 3rd row as before, cont in st st with A only until sleeve measures 43(45,47)cm [17(17¾,18½)in] from beg. Cast off loosely.

NECK INSET AND COLLAR

With rs facing, sl first 20 sts from holder onto a 4½mm needle, join in A and cast on 6 sts for overwrap [26 sts].

Row 1: (rs) K6, (k1, p1) to end.
Row 2: (K1, p1) to last 6 sts, p6.
Keeping border of 6 sts in st st throughout and rem sts in rib, work 4 more rows.

Buttonholes K2, cast off 3, work to end. Next row: Work to end, cast on 3 sts at buttonhole. Work 8 rows. Rep the 2 buttonhole rows then work 2 more rows, so ending ws row. Sew row-ends of inset to right-hand side of neck, then join shoulder seams.

Next row Cast off 6, rib to end, then with same needle holding rem 20 sts, puk 23(25,27) sts from right front neck, k back neck sts from holder, then turn and cast on 43(45,47) sts [106(110,114) sts]. Work 14cm [5½in] for collar in k1, p1 rib. Cast off ribwise.

FINISHING OFF

Sew sleeves to main part, matching centre of each sleeve top with shoulder seam, join side and sleeve seams. Sew cast-on edge of collar to left-hand side of neck (easing it in to fit), ending to correspond with beg of collar on right-hand side of neck. Sew base of overwrap in position and sew on buttons to correspond with buttonholes. Seams may be pressed with hot iron and damp cloth, but do not press ribs.

ROSES

**Needs some experience

SIZE
To fit bust 87-92(92-98,98-104)cm [34-36(36-38,38-40)in]

MATERIALS
Yarn used in sample
Anne Rowena Mohair
Quantities
Main colour (taupe) 13 x 25g balls (A)
1st contrast (red) 3 x 25g balls (B)
2nd contrast (orange) 3 x 25g balls (C)
3rd contrast (emerald) 3 x 25g balls (D)
4th contrast (jade) 2 x 25g balls (E)
5th contrast (brown) 1 x 25g ball (F)
Alternative yarn
Any mohair that knits to same tension
Needles
1 pair each 4½mm (7) and 5½mm (5) needles
1 cable needle for rib

TENSION
Using 5½mm (5) needles over stocking stitch, 14 sts x 18/20 rows = 10 x 10cm [4 x 4in] (see Tension, page 11).

BACK
Rib With 4½mm needles and A, cast on 57(63,69) sts and work rib as folls:
Row 1: *P1(0,1); (k1, p1) 4(6,7) times*; [k1, c2b, k1, c2f, k1; (p1, k1) 4 times, p1] 3 times; rib to end.
Row 2: *K1(0,1); (p1, k1) 4(6,7) times*; [p7, (k1, p1) 4 times, k1] 3 times; rib to end.
Row 3: As row 1 * to *; [c2b, k3, c2f, (p1, k1) 4 times, p1] 3 times; rib to end.
Row 4: As row 2.
Row 5: As row 1 * to *; [k7, (p1, k1) 4 times, p1] 3 times; rib to end.
Row 6: As row 2.
Row 7: As row 1 * to *; [c2f, k3, c2b, (p1, k1) 4 times, p1] 3 times; rib to end.
Row 8: As row 2.
Row 9: As row 1 * to *; [k1, c2f, k1, c2b, k1, (p1, k1) 4 times, p1] 3 times; rib to end.
Row 10: As row 2 * to *; [p1, k1, p3, k1, p1; (k1, p1) 4 times, k1] 3 times; rib to end.
Row 11: As row 1 * to *; [k1, p1 c3f, p1, k1; (p1, k1) 4 times, p1] 3 times;

rib to end.
Row 12: As row 10.
These 12 rows form rib patt. Rep from row 1 to row 11.
Inc row Work as row 12 but work inc sts in as folls. Small: inc in 1st st; (rib 1, inc in next st) 28 times [86 sts]. Medium & Large: rib 2 (5); (rib 1, inc in next st) 29 times; rib to end [92(98) sts]. Change to 5½mm needles. Foll chart as given for back. Work until back measures 67(70,73)cm [26¼(27½,28¾)in] from beg.
Shoulder shaping Cast off 8(9,10) sts at beg of next 2 rows, cast off 9(10,11) sts at beg of foll 4 rows. Leave rem 34 sts on st holder/spare yrn.

FRONT
As for back, but work from chart given for front. When work measures 60(63,66)cm [23½(24¾,26)in] from beg, shape for neck.
Neck shaping Patt first 33(36,39) sts, turn and dec 1 st at beg of next row and every foll alt row to

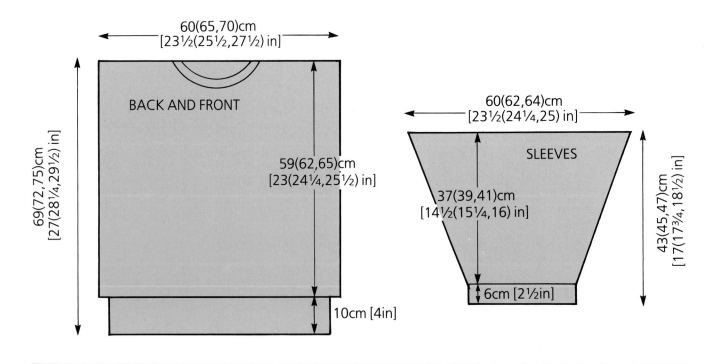

60(65,70)cm
[23½(25½,27½) in]

BACK AND FRONT

69(72,75)cm
[27(28¼,29½) in]

59(62,65)cm
[23(24¼,25½) in]

10cm [4in]

60(62,64)cm
[23½(24¼,25) in]

SLEEVES

37(39,41)cm
[14½(15¼,16) in]

43(45,47)cm
[17(17¾,18½) in]

6cm [2½in]

BACK AND SLEEVES

These 40 rows form pattern and are repeated

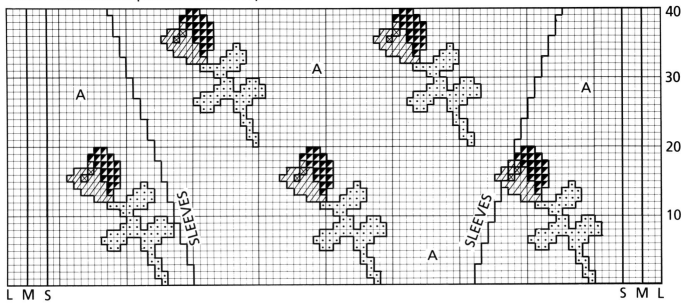

⊠ = F
⊡   D
⊠   B
◨   C

26(29,32) sts. Cont straight until front measures 67(70,73)cm [26¼(27½,28¾)in] from beg.
Shoulder shaping Cast off 8(9,10) sts at beg of next row, work 1 row. Cast off 9(10,11) sts at beg of next and foll alt row. Thread centre 20 sts onto st holder and work rem 33 (36,39) sts to match left side, reversing all shapings.

SLEEVES

Rib With 4½mm needles and A, cast on 31 sts and work rib as for back starting thus:
Row 1: (K1, p1) 6 times; k1, c2b, k1, c2f, k1; (p1, k1) 4 times, p1; rib to end.
Now work as given for back on sts as set. Work 11 rows.
Inc row Work as for 12th row but inc as folls: rib 4; (inc in next st, rib 1) 11 times; rib to end [42 sts]. Change to 5½mm needles. Foll chart as shown for sleeves.
Shaping Inc 1 st each end of 4th and every foll 3rd row until sleeve measures 45(47,49)cm

[17(17¾,18½)in] from beg. Cast off loosely.

NECKBAND

Join left shoulder using backstitch so that no cast-off sts are visible. With rs facing, using 4½mm needles and A, puk 34 sts from back, 14 sts down side, 20 sts from front and 14 sts up side [82 sts]. Work rib as for back starting thus, ws facing: k1; [p7, (k1, p1) 4 times, k1] 5 times; p1. Now work from row 3 to row 12 as for back on sts as set, then a further 8 rows of patt. Cast off patternwise, loosely. Join right shoulder and neckband, fold in half inwards and sew down inside.

FINISHING OFF

Press all pieces using hot iron and damp cloth. Sew in sleeves, matching centre of each sleeve top with shoulder seam. Press these seams. Sew side and sleeve seams, using backstitch or invisible grafting st. Press rem seams, but do not press ribs.

FRONT ONLY

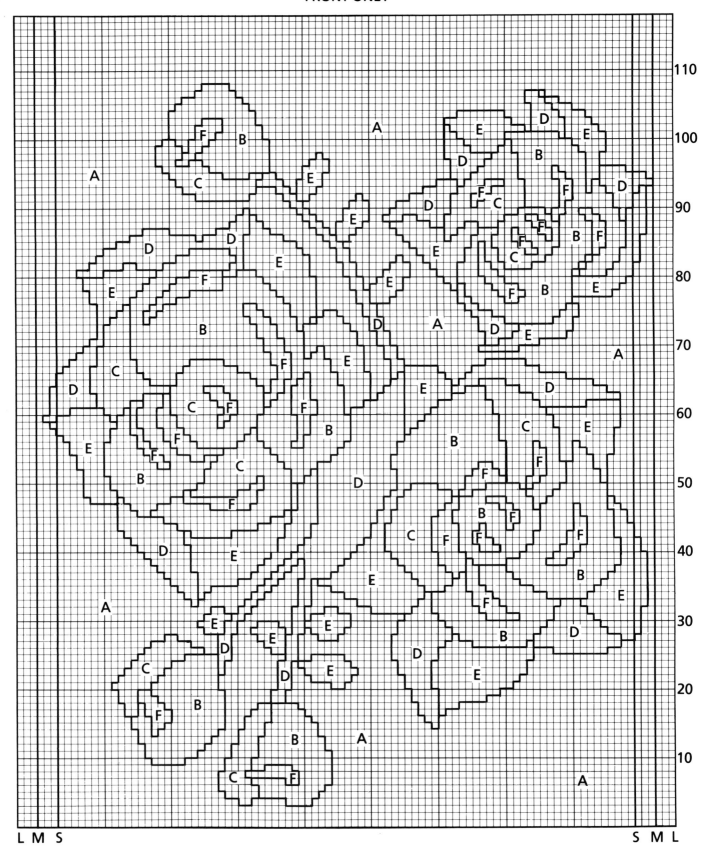

FLOWER BORDER

*Easy

SIZE
To fit bust 87-92(92-98,98-104)cm
[34-36(36-38,38-40)in]

MATERIALS
Yarn used in sample
Anne Rowena Mohair
Quantities
Main colour (natural) 8 x 25g balls (A)
1st contrast (taupe) 9 x 25g balls (B)
2nd contrast (black) 3 x 25g balls (C)
3rd contrast (jade) 1 x 25g ball (D)
4th contrast (royal) 1 x 25g ball (E)
5th contrast (fuchsia) 1 x 25g ball (F)
Alternative yarn
Any mohair that knits up to same
tension
Needles
1 pair each 4½mm (7) and 5½mm
(5) needles
Buttons
3 x 25mm [1in] domes

TENSION
Using 5½mm (5) needles over
stocking stitch, 14 sts x 18/20 rows =
10 x 10cm [4 x 4in] (see Tension,
page 11).

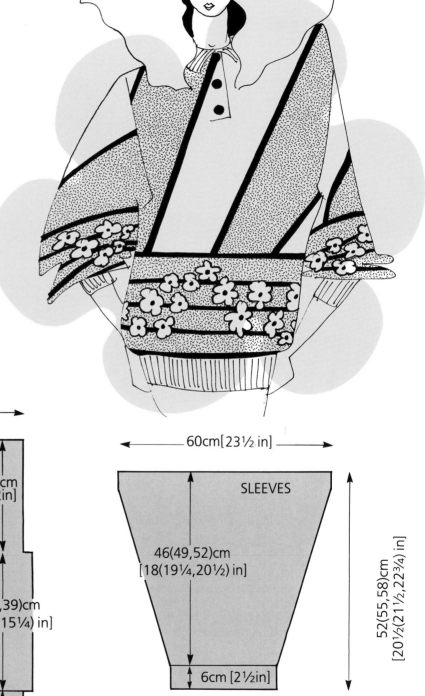

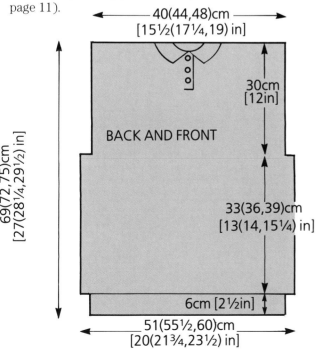

BACK AND FRONT

40(44,48)cm
[15½(17¼,19) in]

30cm
[12in]

33(36,39)cm
[13(14,15¼) in]

69(72,75)cm
[27(28¼,29½) in]

6cm [2½in]

51(55½,60)cm
[20(21¾,23½) in]

SLEEVES

60cm[23½ in]

46(49,52)cm
[18(19¼,20½) in]

52(55,58)cm
[20½(21½,22¾) in]

6cm [2½in]

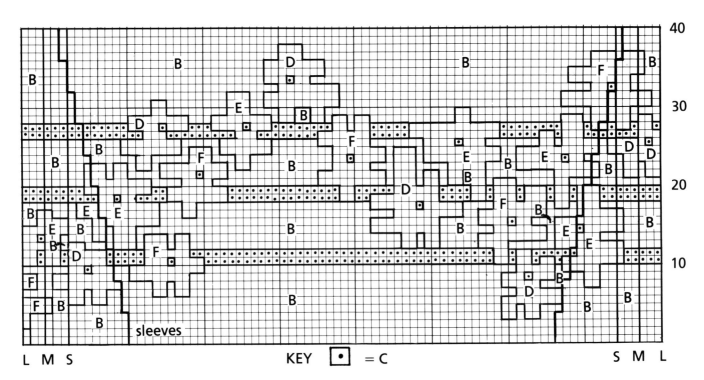

L M S   KEY ▣ = C   S M L

BACK

Rib With 4½mm needles and A, cast on 62(66,70) sts and work k1, p1 rib for 6cm [2½in].

Inc row Inc to 72(78,84) sts evenly over next row. Change to 5½mm needles. Work chart sequence: work 2 rows st st with C. Foll chart for 40 rows. Work 2 rows st st with C.

Diagonal stripes

Row 1: K20A, 2C, 20B, 2C, 20A, 2C, 6(12,18)B.

Row 2: P6(12,18)B, 2C, 20A, 2C, 20B, 2C, 20A.

Row 3: K19A, 2C, 20B, 2C, 20A, 2C, 7(13,19)B.

Row 4: P7(13,19)B, 2C, 20A, 2C, 20B, 2C, 19A.

Cont in this way moving over 1 st each k row. Bring in next stripes when sts allow.

Cont until back measures 39(42,45)cm [15¼(16½,17¾)in] from beg.

Armhole shaping Cast off 8 sts at beg of next 2 rows*. Work straight for a further 30cm [12in], keeping patt correct.

Shoulder shaping Cast off 14(17,20) sts at beg of next 2 rows.

Leave rem 28 sts on st holder/spare yrn.

FRONT

As for back to *.

Neck opening Work further 5cm [2in]. K first 28(31,34) sts only and turn. Cast on 4 sts at beg of next row (buttonband). Work over these 33(35,38) sts, keeping patt correct, until front opening measures 17cm [6¾in], ending with a k row.

Neck shaping Cast off 10 sts at beg of next row. Cast off 2 sts at neck edge on next 2 rows and 1 st at neck edge of foll 4 rows [14(17,20) sts]. Work straight to match back length. Cast off 14(17,20) sts. Work right side to match, cast on 4 sts at neck-edge opening for buttonhole band. Work 4 rows.

Buttonholes K3, yrn fwd, k2tog. Work to end. Next row: p. Work 2 more buttonholes 12 rows apart. Cont with right side to match left side, reversing shapings.

SLEEVES

Rib With 4½mm needles and A, cast on 30 sts and work k1, p1 rib for 6cm

[2½in].

Inc row Rib 2; (inc in next st) 26 times; rib to end [56 sts]. Change to 5½mm needles. Work chart sequence as for back but at the same time inc 1 st each end of 5th and foll 4th rows to 86 sts. Work stripes as for back, starting with 20A, 2C, 20B, 2C, 8B etc. Work to 52(55,58)cm [20½(21½,22¾)in] from beg. Cast off loosely. (The sleeve top must fit in between the armhole shapings on front and back.)

COLLAR

Join both shoulders using backstitch so that no cast-off sts are visible. With rs facing, using 4½mm needles and A, puk 25 sts from beg of buttonhole band to shoulder seam, 28 sts from back, 25 sts down left side (78 sts). Work 10cm [4in] k1, p1 rib. Cast off loosely, ribwise.

FINISHING OFF

Sew in sleeves, setting cast-off edge square into armhole shaping (see p58). Sew side and sleeve seams. Sew buttons in place. Press seams using a damp cloth, but do not press ribs.

MOHAIR CABLE

*Easy

SIZE
To fit bust 87-92(92-98,98-104)cm [34-36(36-38,38-40)in]

MATERIALS
Yarn used in sample
Anne Rowena Mohair
Quantity
22(23,24) x 25g balls
Alternative yarn
Any mohair that knits up to same tension
Needles
1 pair each 6mm (4) and 7mm (2) needles, 1 cable needle

TENSION
Using 7mm (2) needles over stocking stitch, 12 sts x 15 rows = 10 x 10cm [4 x 4in] (see Tension, page 11).

CABLE PATTERN [16 sts]
Row 1: (rs) K.
Row 2 and every ws row: P.
Rows 3 and 5: K.
Row 7: c16f (sl next 8 sts onto cable needle and hold in front, k8, then k8 from cable needle).
Rows 9, 11, 13, 15: K.
Row 16: P.
These 16 rows form patt and are repeated and positioned as indicated below.

BACK
Rib Using 6mm needles, cast on 67(69,71) sts. Work k1, p1 rib for 8cm [3in] ending with rs row.
Inc row Rib 1, (make 1 st by picking up the loop lying before next st and knitting into back of it, rib 1) 10(11,12) times; (m1, rib 2) 23 times; (m1, rib 1) 10(11,12) times [110(114,118) sts]. Change to 7mm needles and work cable patt panels as folls:
1st row (rs): P2(4,4); [1st row of cable patt, p2(2,3)] 5 times; 1st row of cable patt; p2(4,3).
2nd row (ws): K2(4,3); [2nd row of cable patt, p2(2,3)] 5 times; 2nd row of cable patt; k2(4,4). Cont in patt on sts as set until work measures 67(70,73)cm [26½(27½,28¾)in] from beg, ending with ws row.
Shoulder shaping (rs) Patt 50(51,52) sts, turn and leave rem sts on spare needle. Cast off 7 sts at beg of next and foll alt row. Cast off rem 36(37,38) sts. With rs facing, sl next 10 (12,14) sts onto holder for centre back, rejoin yrn to rem sts and complete to match first side, reversing shapings.

FRONT
As for back until work measures 60(63,66)cm [23½(24¾,26)in] from beg.
Neck shaping Patt 50(51,52) sts, turn and leave rem sts on a spare needle. Cast off 4 sts at beg of next and foll 2 alt rows. Patt 1 row, then dec 1 st at beg of next and foll alt row to 36(37,38) sts. Cont until front measures same as back to shoulder shaping. Cast off. With rs facing, sl next 10(12,14) sts onto a holder for centre front, rejoin yrn to rem sts and complete to match first side, reversing all shapings.

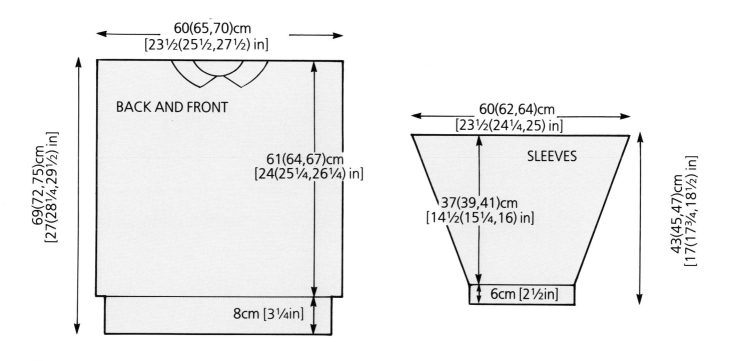

60(65,70)cm [23½(25½,27½) in]

BACK AND FRONT

61(64,67)cm [24(25¼,26¼) in]

69(72,75)cm [27(28¼,29½) in]

8cm [3¼in]

60(62,64)cm [23½(24¼,25) in]

SLEEVES

37(39,41)cm [14½(15¼,16) in]

43(45,47)cm [17(17¾,18½) in]

6cm [2½in]

SLEEVES

Rib With 6mm needles, cast on 36 sts and work k1, p1 rib for 6cm [2½in].
Inc row (rib 1, m1) to end [54 sts].
Change to 7mm needles and work cable patt as folls:
Row 1 (rs): P1; (1st row of cable patt, p2) twice; 1st row of cable patt; p1.
Row 2 (ws): K1; (2nd row of cable patt, k2) twice; 2nd row of cable patt; k1.
Cont in patt on sts as set at the same time inc 1 st each end of 5th and every foll 4th row to 90 sts, bringing in cable patt as extra sts allow. Work straight until sleeve measures 43(45,47)cm [17(17¾,18½)in] from beg. Cast off loosely.

NECKBAND

Join right shoulder seam using backstitch so that no cast-off sts are visible. With rs facing and 6mm needles, puk 14 sts down left-front neck shaping, k across 10(12,14) sts at centre front, puk 14 sts up right-front neck shaping, 11 sts down right-back shaping, k across 10(12,14) sts at centre back, then puk 11 sts up left-back shaping [70(74,78) sts]. Work k1 p1 rib for 2½cm [1in]. Cast off ribwise.

COLLAR

Using 6mm needles, cast on 72(76,80) sts and work in k1, p1 rib for 14cm [5½in]. Cast off loosely and evenly ribwise.

FINISHING OFF

Join left shoulder and neckband seam. Sew in sleeves, matching centre of cast-off edge of each sleeve to shoulder seam. Join side and sleeve seams. Sew collar to inside of neckband, ensuring that opening lies at centre front and that neckband is free (ie join at pick-up sts of neckband).

TRIANGLES

SIZE
To fit bust 87-92(92-98,98-104)cm
[34-36(36-38,38-40)in]

MATERIALS
Yarn used in sample
Anne Rowena Mohair
Quantities
Main colour (jade) 11 x 25g balls (A)
1st contrast (black) 6 x 25g balls (B)
2nd contrast (grey) 4 x 25g balls C)
Alternative yarn
Any mohair that knits up to same
tension
Needles
1 pair each 4½mm (7) and 5½mm
(5) needles
Buttons
2 x triangular buttons

TENSION
Using 5½mm (5) needles over
stocking stitch, 14 sts x 18/20 rows =
10 x 10cm [4 x 4in] (see Tension,
page 11).

BACK
Rib With 4½mm needles and A, cast
on 70(76,82) sts and work k1, p1 rib
for 5cm [2in], ending with ws row.
Buttonhole Rib 6, cast off 3 sts, rib
to end of row. Next row: Rib to cast-
off sts, cast on 3 sts, rib 6. Cont to rib
until work measures 10cm [4in].
Front flap Cast off first 14 sts, rib to
end of row.
Inc row Small: (inc in next st) twice;
(rib 1, inc in next st) 26 times; (inc in
next st) twice [86 sts]. Medium &
Large: rib 1(4); (rib 1, inc in next st)
30 times; rib to end [92(98) sts].
Change to 5½mm needles.
Now foll chart for back working in st
st, noting beg and end sts for each
size. Use separate balls of yrn for
each block of colour to avoid drawing
yrn across at back. Twist yrn round at
back to prevent holes appearing.
Work until back measures
67(70,73)cm [26½(27½, 29¾)in]
from beg.
Shoulder shaping Cast off 8(9,10)
sts at beg of next 2 rows, cast off

9(10,11) sts at beg of foll 4 rows.
Leave rem 34 sts on st holder/spare
yrn.

FRONT
Rib With 4½mm needles and A, cast
on 56(62,68) sts and work k1, p1 rib
for 10cm [4in].
Inc row As for back. Change to
5½mm needles. Foll chart for front
until work measures 60(63,66)cm
[23½(24¾,26)in] from beg.
Neck shaping Patt first 33(36,39)
sts, turn. Dec 1 st at beg of next and
every foll alt row to 26(29,32) sts.
Cont straight until front measures
same as back.
Shoulder shaping Cast off 8(9,10)
sts at beg of next row, work 1 row.
Cast off 9(10,11) sts at beg of next
and foll alt row. Thread centre 20 sts
onto st holder and work rem
33(36,39) sts to match left side,
reversing shapings.

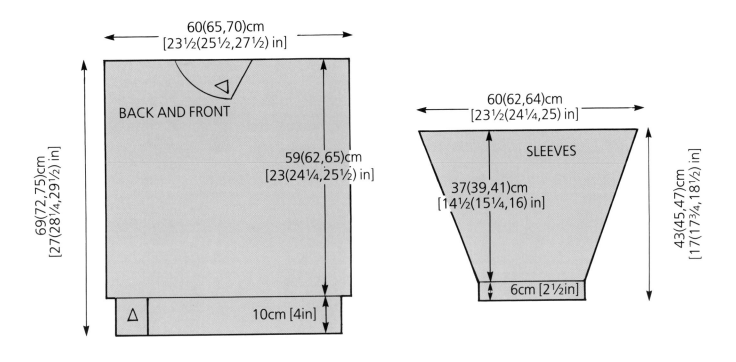

60(65,70)cm
[23½(25½,27½) in]

BACK AND FRONT

69(72,75)cm
[27(28¼,29½) in]

59(62,65)cm
[23(24¼,25½) in]

10cm [4in]

60(62,64)cm
[23½(24¼,25) in]

SLEEVES

37(39,41)cm
[14½(15¼,16) in]

43(45,47)cm
[17(17¾,18½) in]

6cm [2½in]

SLEEVES

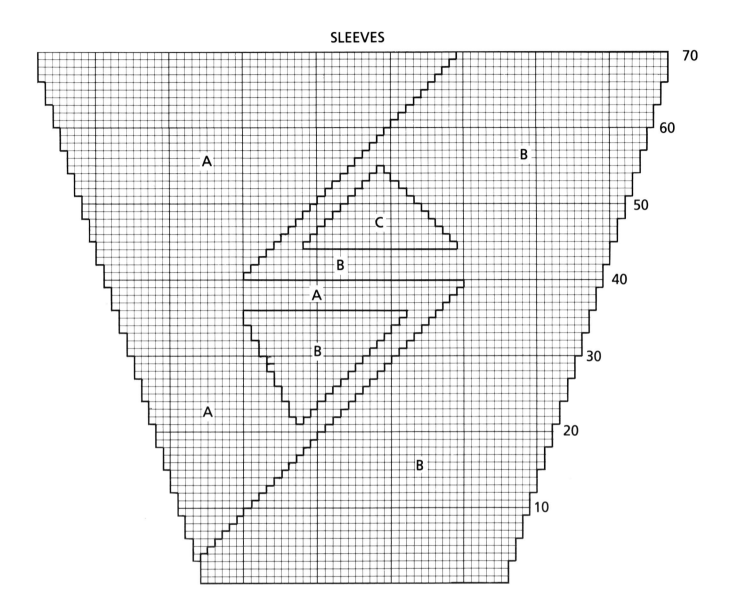

SLEEVES

Rib With 4½mm needles and A, cast on 30 sts and work k1, p1 rib for 6cm [2½in].

Inc row Rib 3; (inc in next st, rib 1) 12 times; rib to end [42 sts]. Change to 5½mm needles and foll charts given for sleeves.

Shaping Inc 1 st each end of 4th and every foll 3rd row (4th, 7th, 10th etc) to end. When sleeve measures 43(45,47)cm [17(17¾, 18½)in] from beg, cast off loosely.

COLLAR

Join right shoulder, using backstitch so that no cast-off sts are visible. With rs facing and using 4½mm needles and A, puk 14 sts down left side, 20 sts across front, 14 sts up right side and 34 sts from back [82 sts]. Work k1, p1 rib for 17cm [6¾in] ending so that front, rs of jumper, is facing.

Buttonhole Rib 6, cast off 3 sts, rib to end. Next row: Rib 73, cast on 3 sts, rib 6. Cont to rib normally until collar measures 20cm [8in]. Cast off ribwise.

FINISHING OFF

Join left shoulder using backstitch. Cont to sew 5cm [2in] of collar ensuring that collar seam is on inside when collar folds over shoulder. Sew in sleeves, using backstitch, matching centre of each sleeve top with shoulder seam. Sew side and sleeve seams. Seams may be pressed using hot iron and damp cloth, but do not press ribs. Sew on buttons to correspond with buttonholes.

FRONT AND BACK

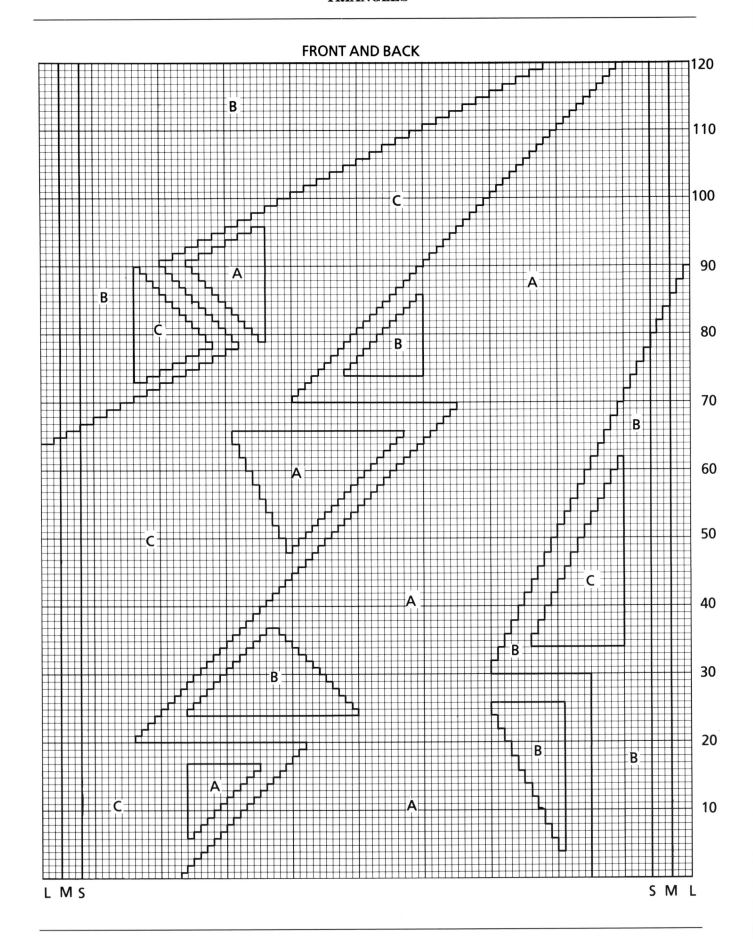

MOHAIR JACKET

*Easy

SIZE
To fit bust 87-104cm [34-40in]

MATERIALS
Yarn used in sample
Anne Rowena Mohair
Quantity
24 x 25g balls
Alternative yarn
Any mohair that knits up to same tension
Needles
1 pair each 4½mm (7) and 5½mm (5) needles
Buttons
6 x 37mm [1½in] domes

TENSION
Using 5½mm (5) needles over stocking stitch, 14 sts x 18/20 rows = 10 x 10cm [4 x 4in] (see Tension, page 11).

BACK
Rib With 4½mm needles, cast on 62 sts and work k2, p2 rib for 10cm [4in].

Inc row Rib 1; (rib 1, inc in next st) 30 times, rib to end [92 sts]. Change to 5½mm needles. Work straight st st until work measures 65cm [25½in] from beg. Cast off loosely.

FRONTS
Pocket linings (2) With 5½mm needles, cast on 24 sts and work 24 rows. Sl sts onto spare needle.
Left front With 4½mm needles, cast on 44 sts and work k2, p2 rib for 10cm [4in]. Change to 5½mm needles. Work straight st st for 24 rows. Next row: K first 10 sts, leave centre 24 sts on holder and work 24 sts of pocket lining in their place; then work rem 10 sts. Cont with front until work measures 40cm [15½in] from beg.
Neck shaping Dec 1 st at neck edge on rows 1, 3 and 5, then on every 4th row to 32 sts. Work straight to match back length. Cast off loosely.
Right front As for left front, but reverse shapings.

SLEEVES WITH SADDLE SHOULDERS
Rib With 4½mm needles, cast on 30 sts and work k2, p2 rib for 6cm [2½in].
Inc row Rib 3; (inc in next st, rib 1) 12 times; rib to end [42 sts]. Change to 5½mm needles and work in st st shaping sleeves by inc 1 st each end of 4th and every foll 3rd row. Cont until there are 88 sts and sleeve measures 45cm [17¾in] from beg.
Saddle shoulders Cast off 29 sts at beg of next 2 rows. Work straight on rem 30 sts only for a further 22cm [8½in]. (This section must eventually be same length as width of front top, so work to match that.)
Left sleeve Dec 1 st at right-hand side of work every row to 15 sts. Work 5 rows more; cast off.
Right sleeve Dec 1 st at left-hand side of work and cont as for left sleeve.

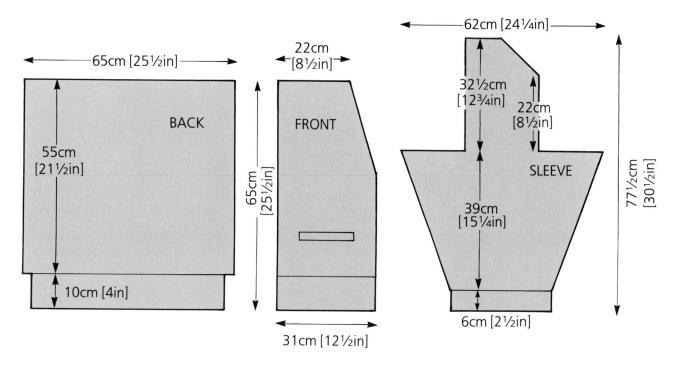

65cm [25½in]

BACK

55cm [21½in]

10cm [4in]

22cm [8½in]

FRONT

65cm [25½in]

31cm [12½in]

62cm [24¼in]

32½cm [12¾in]

22cm [8½in]

SLEEVE

39cm [15¼in]

77½cm [30½in]

6cm [2½in]

COLLAR

Right front With rs facing, using 4½mm needles, puk 112 sts from beg of rib to top. Work 3 rows k2, p2 rib.
Buttonholes Rib 3; (cast off 3, rib 7) 5 times; cast off 3, rib to end. Next row: Rib, but cast on 3 sts over those cast off in previous row. Change to 5½mm needles and rib 1 row.
Revers Rib 2, turn, rib to end. Rib 4, turn, rib to end. Rib 6, turn, rib to end. Cont in this way until the row 'rib 48, turn, rib to end' has been worked. Rib 1 row across all sts. Cast off loosely, ribwise.
Left front Puk 112 sts along front edge and work 6 rows rib. Change to 5½mm needles and work 1 row rib (ending at top end of front). Work rever as for right side. Cast off loosely, ribwise.
Back collar Join saddle shoulders at centre back and sew in back and front between cast-off edges of sleeves and saddle shoulders. With rs facing, using 4½mm needles, puk 40 sts between left and right fronts. P 1 row, inc 1 st every other st to 60 sts. Work in k2, p2 rib for 8 rows. Change to 5½mm needles and work to match rever length. Cast off loosely, ribwise. Sew collar seams together as neatly as possible.

FINISHING OFF

Sew side and sleeve seams. Sew on buttons to correspond with buttonholes.
Pocket tops With 4½mm needles pick up 24 sts on holder and work 6 rows k2, p2 rib. Cast off loosely, ribwise. Neatly sew pocket tops to outside of jacket fronts and sew pocket linings down inside jacket. Press seams gently with a hot iron and damp cloth, but do not press ribs.

Sew saddle shoulders in place thus

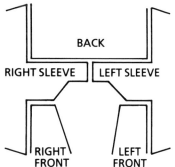

WOOLLY JUMPER

**Needs some experience

SIZE
To fit bust 87-92(92-98,98-104)cm [34-36(36-38,38-40)in]

MATERIALS
Yarn used in sample
Anne Rowena Mohair
Quantities
Main colour (white) 10 x 25g balls (A)
1st contrast (grey) 8 x 25g balls (B)
2nd contrast (red) 5 x 25g balls C)
Alternative yarn
Any mohair that knits up to same tension
Needles
1 pair each 4½mm (7) and 5½mm (5) needles

TENSION
Using 5½mm (5) needles over stocking stitch, 14 sts x 18/20 rows = 10 x 10cm [4 x 4in] (see Tension, page 11).

BACK
Rib With 4½mm needles and A, cast on 56(62,68) sts and work k1, p1 rib for 10cm [4in].
Inc row Small: (inc in next st) twice; (rib 1, inc in next st) 26 times; (inc in next st) twice [86 sts]. Medium & Large: rib 1(4); (rib 1, inc in next st) 30 times; rib to end [92(98) sts]. Change to 5½mm needles.
Now foll chart for back working in st st, noting beg and end sts for each size. Use separate balls of yrn for each block of colour to avoid drawing yrn across at back. Twist yrn round at back to prevent holes appearing. Work until back measures 62(65,68)cm [24½(25½,26¾)in] from beg.
Shoulder shaping Cast off 8(9,10) sts at beg of next 2 rows, cast off 9(10,11) sts at beg of foll 4 rows. Cast off rem 34 sts.

FRONT
As for back but work to 55(58,61)cm [21½(23,24)in] from beg.
Neck shaping Patt first 33(36,39) sts, turn and dec 1 st at beg of next and every foll alt row to 26(29,32) sts. Cont straight until front measures 62(65,68)cm [24½(25½,26¾)in] from beg.
Shoulder shaping Cast off 8(9,10) sts at beg of next row, work 1 row. Cast off 9(10,11) sts at beg of next and foll alt row. Thread centre 20 sts onto st holder/spare yrn and work rem sts to match left side.

SLEEVES
Rib With 4½mm needles and A, cast on 30 sts and work k1, p1 rib for 6cm [2½in].
Inc row Rib 3; (inc in next st, rib 1) 12 times; rib to end [42 sts]. Change to 5½mm needles and foll charts given for sleeves.
Shaping Inc 1 st each end of 4th and every foll 3rd row (4th, 7th, 10th etc) to end. When sleeve measures 43(45,47)cm [17(17¾,18½)in] from beg, cast off loosely.

COLLAR
With 4½mm needles and C, cast on 40 sts. Work k1, p1 rib for 6cm [2½in].
Slits Rib 10 sts, turn. Work 8 rows on these 10 sts only, ending with sts on right-hand needle. Break yrn and

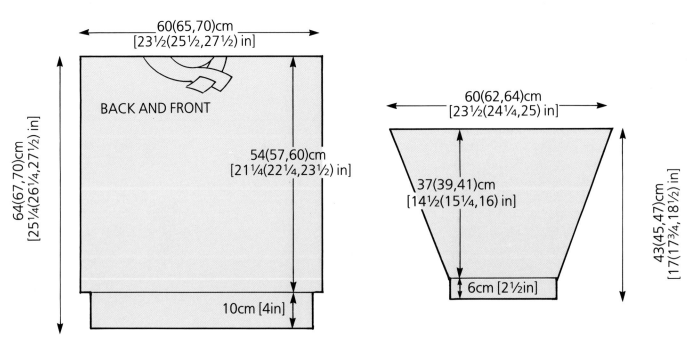

BACK AND FRONT

60(65,70)cm [23½(25½,27½) in]

64(67,70)cm [25¼(26¼,27½) in]

54(57,60)cm [21¼(22¼,23½) in]

10cm [4in]

60(62,64)cm [23½(24¼,25) in]

37(39,41)cm [14½(15¼,16) in]

6cm [2½in]

43(45,47)cm [17(17¾,18½)in]

SLEEVES

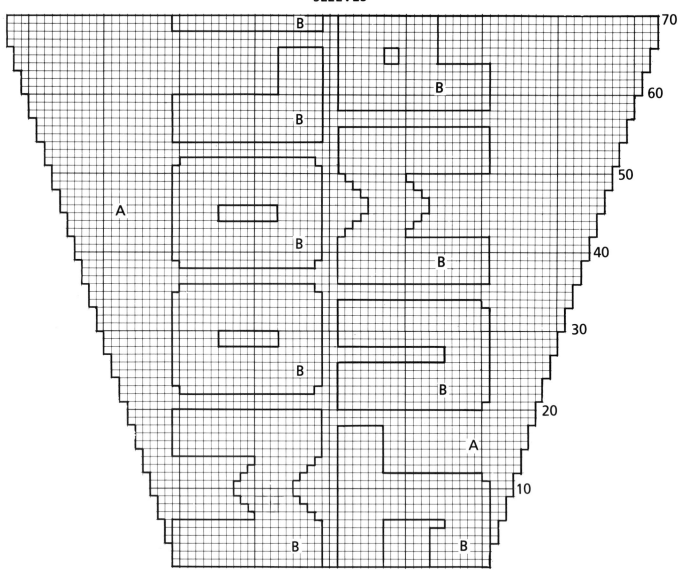

rejoin to rib centre 20 sts only, turn. Work 8 rows. Break yrn and rejoin to work rem 10 sts in same way. Now rib 1 row across all 40 sts. Cont to rib until collar measures 75cm [29½in] from beg. Cast off ribwise.

FINISHING OFF

Join both shoulders, using backstitch so that no cast-off sts are visible. Pin collar round neck as folls. Mark 10cm [4in] from each end of collar. Pin middle 55cm [21½in] of collar round neck opening, starting at the bottom left side, up towards back, pin along back, down right side, then along front. You may have to ease neck edge to fit. Make sure end with slits is at the front. Sew collar onto jumper using invisible sts, so that no seam is visible from either direction. Fold collar in half outwards and push end of collar through slits.

Sew collar on thus

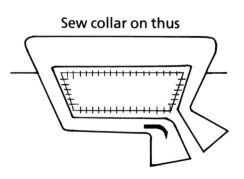

BACK AND FRONT

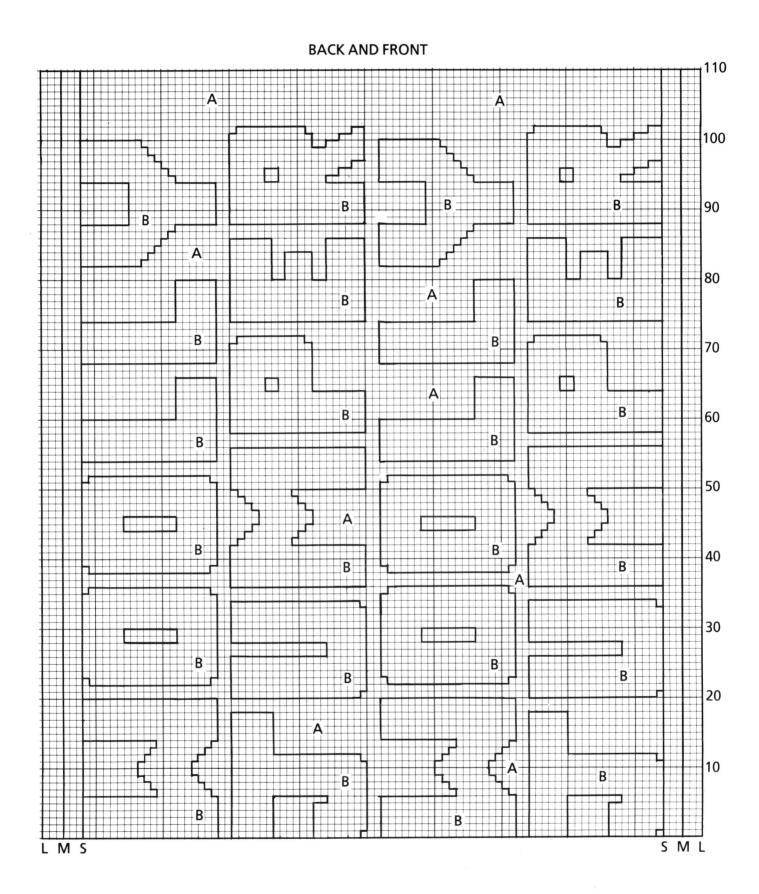

FLOWER SQUARES

**Needs some experience

SIZE
To fit bust 87-92(92-98,98-104)cm [34-36(36-38,38-40)in]

MATERIALS
Yarn used in sample
Anne Rowena Mohair
Quantities
Main colour (navy) 12 x 25g balls (A)
1st contrast (fuchsia) 2 x 25g balls (B)
2nd contrast (red) 2 x 25g balls (C)
3rd contrast (purple) 2 x 25g balls (D)
4th contrast (jade) 2 x 25g balls (E)
5th contrast (gold) 2 x 25g balls (F)
6th contrast (royal) 2 x 25g balls (G)
Alternative yarn
Any mohair that knits up to same tension
Needles
1 pair each 4½mm (7) and 5½mm (5) needles
Buttons
8 x 25mm [1in] domes

TENSION
Using 5½mm (5) needles over stocking stitch, 14 sts x 18/20 rows = 10 x 10cm [4 x 4in] (see Tension, page 11).

BACK
Rib With 4½mm needles and A, cast on 56(62,68) sts and work k1, p1 rib for 10cm [4in].
Inc row Small: (inc in next st) twice; (rib 1, inc in next st) 26 times; (inc in next st) twice [86 sts]. Medium & Large: rib 1(4); (rib 1, inc in next st) 30 times; rib to end [92(98) sts], Change to 5½mm needles.
Chart sequence for back
Rows 1-56(58,60): Work 43(46,49) sts of chart using 1st colourway followed by 43(46,49) sts of chart using 2nd colourway.
Rows 57(59,61) to end: Work 43(46,49) sts of chart using 2nd colourway, followed by 43(46,49) sts of chart using 1st colourway. If more rows are required, work plain A. Work until back measures 67(70,73)cm [26¼(27½,28¾)in] from beg.
Shoulder shaping Cast off 8(9,10) sts at beg of next 2 rows, cast off 9(10,11) sts at beg of foll 4 rows. Leave rem 34 sts on st holder/spare yrn.

LEFT FRONT
Rib With 4½mm needles and A, cast on 40(43,46) sts and work 10cm [4in] k1, p1 rib, inc 3 sts evenly over last row [43(46,49) sts]. Change to 5½mm needles.
Chart sequence for left front
Rows 1-56(58-60): Work chart in 1st colourway.
Rows 57(59,61) to end: Work chart in 2nd colourway.
Work until front measures 60(63,66)cm [23½(24¾,26)in] from beg, ending with a k row.
Neck shaping Sl first 10 sts onto safety pin, work to end. Dec 1 st at neck edge of next and every foll alt row to 26(29,32) sts. Cont straight until front measures 67(70,73)cm [26¼(27½,28¾)in] from beg.
Shoulder shaping Cast off 8(9,10) sts at beg of next row, work 1 row. Cast off 9(10,11) sts at beg of next and foll alt row.

RIGHT FRONT
Work as for left but work first chart repeat in 2nd colourway and second chart repeat in 1st colourway. Reverse all shapings.

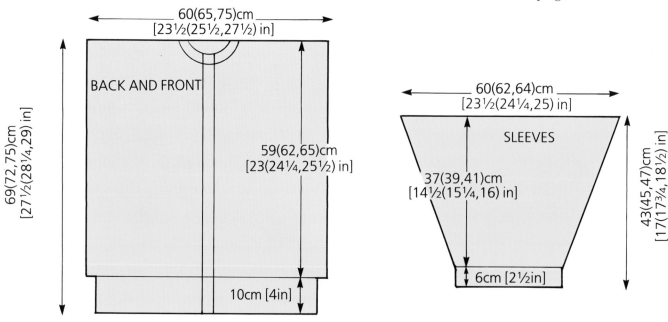

BACK AND FRONT

60(65,75)cm [23½(25½,27½) in]

69(72,75)cm [27½(28¼,29) in]

59(62,65)cm [23(24¼,25½) in]

10cm [4in]

SLEEVES

60(62,64)cm [23½(24¼,25) in]

37(39,41)cm [14½(15¼,16) in]

43(45,47)cm [17(17¾,18½) in]

6cm [2½in]

SLEEVES

Rib With 4½mm needles and A, cast on 30 sts and work k1, p1 rib for 6cm [2½in].
Inc row Rib 3; (inc in next st, rib 1) 12 times; rib to end [42 sts]. Change to 5½mm needles.
Chart sequence for sleeves
Both sleeves the same.
Row 1: Work last 21 sts of chart using 1st colourway, followed by first 21 sts of chart using 2nd colourway. Working on these sts as set, complete the charts, at the same time shape sleeve thus: inc 1 st each end of 4th and every foll 3rd row (4th, 7th, 10th etc) until sleeve measures 43(45,47)cm [17(17¾,18½)in] from beg. Cast off loosely.

FRONT BANDS

Buttonband (left side) With 4½mm needles and A, cast on 7 sts and work k1, p1 rib until band measures from beg of rib to beg of neck shaping when slightly stretched. Sl the 7 sts onto safety pin. Graft band in place and sew 7 buttons in place evenly spaced out along band.
Buttonhole band (right side) As for buttonband but make buttonholes to correspond with button placings.
Buttonholes Rib 3, yrn fwd, k2tog, rib 2; next row rib. When band complete, sl sts onto safety pin, and graft in place.
Neckband Join both shoulders using backstitch so that no cast-off sts are visible. With rs facing, using 4½mm needles and A, starting with right band, puk 7 sts from band, 10 sts from safety pin, 14 sts up side, 34 sts from back, 14 sts down side, 10 sts from safety pin and 7 sts from other band [96 sts]. Work 8cm [3in] k1, p1 rib making 2 buttonholes on right side at 2cm [¾in] and 6cm [2½in]. Cast off loosely, ribwise, fold band in half inwards, placing buttonholes over each other to make a single hole and sew band down. Sew on button.

CHART FOR FLOWER SQUARES

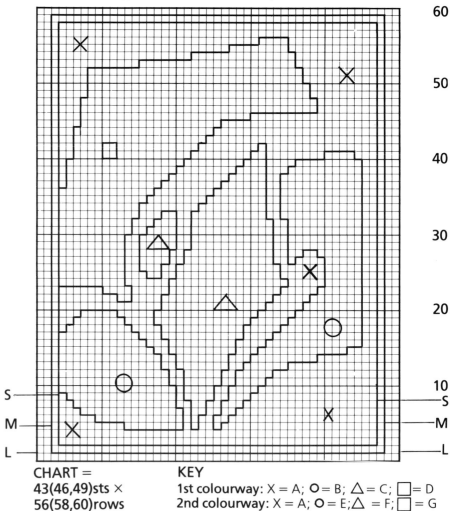

CHART = 43(46,49)sts × 56(58,60)rows

KEY
1st colourway: X = A; O = B; △ = C; ☐ = D
2nd colourway: X = A; O = E; △ = F; ☐ = G

SLEEVES

1ST	2ND
2ND C/WAY	1ST C/WAY

BACK AND FRONTS

1ST C/WAY	2ND C/WAY
2ND C/WAY	1ST C/WAY

FINISHING OFF

Sew in sleeves, matching centre of each sleeve top with shoulder seam. Sew side and sleeve seams. Seams may be pressed using hot iron and damp cloth, but do not press ribs.

RAGLAN MOHAIR

*Easy

SIZE
To fit bust 87-92(92-98,98-104)cm
[34-36(36-38,38-40)in]

MATERIALS
Yarn used in sample
Anne Rowena Mohair
Quantity
14(15,16) x 25g balls
Alternative yarn
Any mohair that knits up to same
tension
Needles
1 pair each 4½mm (7) and 5½mm
(5) needles
Buttons
1 large dome

TENSION
Using 5½mm (5) needles over
stocking stitch, 14 sts x 18/20 rows =
10 x 10cm [4 x 4in] (see Tension,
page 11).

NOTES ON PLAIN JUMPERS
For a beginner, a plain mohair jumper
is an ideal start. Once you have

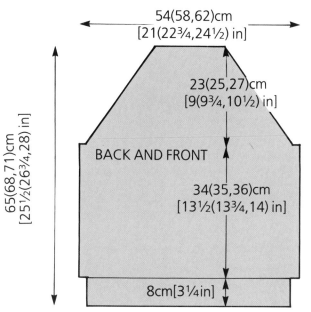

54(58,62)cm
[21(22¾,24½) in]

23(25,27)cm
[9(9¾,10½) in]

BACK AND FRONT

34(35,36)cm
[13½(13¾,14) in]

65(68,71)cm
[25½(26¾,28) in]

8cm[3¼in]

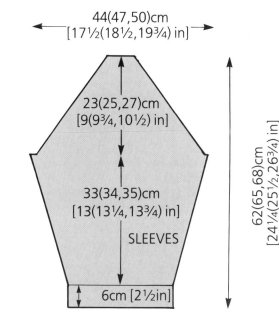

44(47,50)cm
[17½(18½,19¾) in]

23(25,27)cm
[9(9¾,10½) in]

33(34,35)cm
[13(13¼,13¾) in]

SLEEVES

62(65,68)cm
[24¼(25½,26¾) in]

6cm [2½in]

completed your first jumper you then have a perfect 'template' to work from for other ideas. By using the two plain jumpers (here and p57), or the shapes of the other jumpers in the book, omitting the pattern, it is quite easy to add your own designs. Stripes and squares for example, are very easy to do and also use up all sorts of odds and ends. Otherwise, using the charts as a guide, why not work out your own patterns and have your very own 'original'?

BACK

Rib With 4½mm needles, cast on 62(66,70) sts and work k2, p2 rib for 8cm [3¼in].

Inc row Rib 4(2,0); (inc in next st, rib 3) to last 2(0,2) sts; rib 2(0,1 and inc in last st) [76(82,88) sts]. Change to 5½mm needles. Work in st st until back measures 42(43,44)cm [16½(17,17½)in] from beg.

Raglan shaping Cast off 5 sts at beg of next 2 rows. Next row: K2, skpo, k to last 4 sts, k2tog, k2. Next row: P. Rep these 2 rows until 26(28,30) sts rem. Leave these sts on st holder/ spare yrn.

FRONT

As for back until front measures 33(34,35)cm [13(13½,14)in] from beg.

Neck shaping Patt first 30(33,36) sts, turn. Cont to work on these sts only, until work measures 42(43,44)cm [16½(17,17½)in] from beg, ending with a p row.

Raglan shaping Cast off 5 sts at beg of next row. P next row to end. Next row: K2, skpo, k to end. Next row: P. Rep these 2 rows until 13(15,17) sts rem, ending with p row. Now dec 1 st at neck edge every k row, cont to shape raglan as before. Work to 1 st, fasten off.

Right side Cast off centre 16 sts and work rem 30(33,36) sts to match left side, reversing all shapings.

RIGHT SLEEVE

Rib With 4½mm needles and A, cast on 30 sts and work k2, p2 rib for 6cm [2½in].

Inc row Inc in 1st st; (inc in next st, rib 1) to end, inc in last st to make 46 sts. Change to 5½mm needles. Work in st st but at the same time inc 1 st each end of 5th and every foll 4th row to 62(66,70) sts. Work straight until sleeve measures 39(40,41)cm [15¼(15¾,16)in] from beg, ending with a p row.

Raglan shaping Cast off 5 sts at beg of next 2 rows. Next row: K2, skpo, k to last 4 sts, k2tog, k2. Next row: P*. Rep the last 2 rows until 14 sts rem, ending with k row.

Shaping top P to last 4 sts, turn. K next row, keeping raglan shaping correct. Rep these 2 rows once more. P all 12 sts and leave on st holder.

LEFT SLEEVE

As for right sleeve to *.

Shaping top Rep last 2 rows to 14 sts ending with p row. Next row: K (keeping raglan shaping correct) to last 4 sts, turn. Next row: P. Rep these 2 rows once more. Leave rem 12 sts on st holder.

COLLAR

Right side Sew in right sleeve only (back and front seams). With rs facing, using 4½mm needles, puk 48(50,52) sts up front neck edge opening; puk the 12 sts from sleeve and 26(28,30) sts from back thus: [k4(2,1) k2tog] 6(10,14) times [80 sts altogether]. Now work k2, p2 rib for 10 rows.

Buttonhole Rib 68 sts, cast off next 5 sts, rib to end of row. Next row: rib 7, cast on 5 sts, rib to end of row. Work another 8 rows rib [20 rows altogether].

Shaping Rib first 60 sts of next row, turn. Rib to end. Rib 58 sts, turn, rib to end. Rib 56 sts, turn, rib to end. Cont in this way, working 2 sts less each time until 'rib 42 sts, turn, rib to

end'. Cast off all 80 sts, loosely, ribwise.

Left side Sew in front seam of left sleeve only. With ws facing, using 4½mm needles, pup 48(50,52) sts up front neck edge opening; pup the 12 sts from sleeve thus: [p4(1,0), p2tog] 2(4,6) times [58 sts altogether]. Work k2, p2 rib for 20 rows.

Shaping Next row: rib 38 sts, turn, rib to end. Rib 36 sts, turn, rib to end. Cont in this way to 'rib 20 sts', turn, rib to end. Cast off all 58 sts, loosely, ribwise.

FINISHING OFF

Join rem raglan sleeve. Cont the seam up the collar, reversing seam so that ws of collar is face down when jumper is right side out. Sew right collar edge to cast-off edge of front section, making neat seam. Sew left collar at back. Sew side and sleeve seams. Sew button to correspond with buttonhole. Press seams gently with hot iron and damp cloth, but do not press ribs.

BOWS

**Needs some experience

SIZE
To fit bust 87-92(92-98,98-104)cm [34-36(36-38,38-40)in]

MATERIALS
Yarn used in sample
Anne Rowena Mohair
Quantities
Main colour (black) 7 x 25g balls (A)
1st contrast (grey) 6 x 25g balls (B)
2nd contrast (fuchsia) 6 x 25g balls (C)
3rd contrast (white) 3 x 25g balls (D)
Alternative yarn
Any mohair that knits up to same tension
Needles
1 pair each 4½mm (7) and 5½mm (5) needles

TENSION
Using 5½mm (5) needles over stocking stitch, 14 sts x 18/20 rows = 10 x 10cm [4 x 4in] (see Tension, page 11).

BACK
Rib With 4½mm needles and A, cast on 56(62,68) sts and work k1, p1 rib for 10cm [4in].
Inc row Small: (inc in next st) twice; (rib 1, inc in next st) 26 times; (inc in next st) twice [86 sts]. Medium & Large: rib 1(4); (rib 1, inc in next st) 30 times; rib to end [92(98) sts].
Change to 5½mm needles and foll chart thus:
Row 1: Foll 43(46,49) sts from chart reading from right to left, noting beg and end sts and rows for each size, then k43(46,49) sts with A.
Row 2: P43(46,49)A, foll 43(46,49) sts from chart, reading from left to right. Rep these 2 rows until chart is complete, noting end rows for each size.
Next row: K43(46,49)D, 43(46,49)B.
Next row: P43(46,49)B, 43(46,49)D.
Second half:
Row 1: K43(46,49) B, foll 43(46,49) sts from chart, noting different colourway.
Row 2: P43(46,49) sts from chart, p43(46,49)B. Rep these 2 rows until chart is complete.

SHOULDER SHAPING
Shoulder shaping Cast off 26(29,32) sts at beg of next 2 rows. Leave rem 34 sts on st holder/spare yrn.

FRONT
As for back until work measures 8cm [3¼in] less than back.
Neck shaping Patt first 33(36,39) sts, turn and dec 1 st at beg of next row and every foll alt row to 26(29,32) sts. Cont straight until front measures same as back. Cast off. Thread centre 20 sts onto st holder and work rem sts to match left side, reversing shapings.

SLEEVES
Rib With 4½mm needles and A, cast on 30 sts and work k1, p1 rib for 6cm [2½in].
Inc row Rib 3; (inc in next st, rib 1) 12 times; rib to end [42 sts]. Change to 5½mm needles.
Left sleeve pattern
Row 1: K21B, then first 21 sts of chart, using colourways as for second half of back.

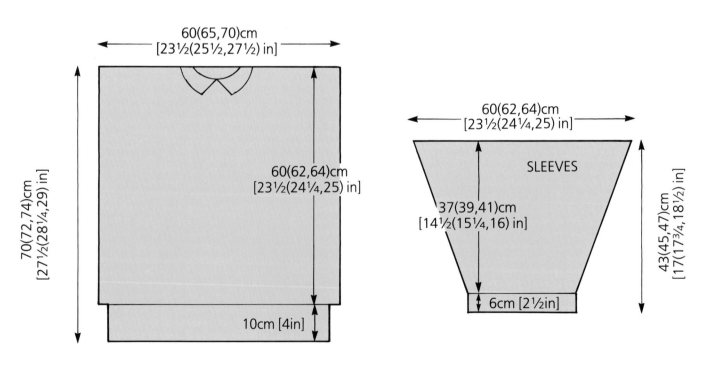

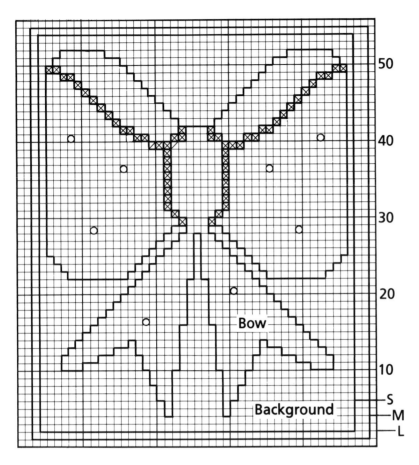

50

40

30

20

10

S
M
L

Bow

Background

KEY
First part of back/front and right sleeve;
    Background – C
    Bow – B
    O – bobble in D
    X – A (use 2 lengths)

2nd part of back/front and left sleeve;
    Background – D
    Bow – C
    O – bobble in A
    X – A

Bobbles – Join 35cms of yarn.
    (k1,p1,k1) all in next st,
    turn. k3,turn, p3, turn. Sl
    1, k2 tog, psso.

Row 2: P the 21 sts from chart, then 21B.
Repeat these 2 rows, at the same time inc 1 st each end of 4th and every foll 3rd row. When chart complete, work next 2 rows thus: K half the row in A, the other half in C. Next row: P in these colours. Now work rem of sleeve thus: 1st half C, 2nd half A. Cont to inc at the sides. Work until sleeve measures 43(45,47)cm [17(17¾,18½in] from beg. Cast off loosely.
Right sleeve pattern
Work as for left sleeve but work chart pattern first, starting at st 21 and using colourways as for first half of back and 2nd 21 sts in A. When chart complete work 2 rows thus: 1st half D, 2nd half B and complete the sleeve with 1st half B, 2nd half D.

NECKBAND AND COLLAR
Join left shoulder using backstitch so that no cast-off sts are visible. With rs facing, using 4½mm needles and A, puk 34 sts from back, 14 sts down side, 20 sts from front and 14 sts up side [82 sts]. Work 4 rows k1, p1 rib. Cast off loosely, ribwise.
Collar With 4½mm needles and C, cast on 84 sts and work 10cm [4in] k1, p1 rib. Cast off loosely, ribwise. Join right shoulder, sew collar inside neckband, loosely, ensuring opening is at centre front of jumper. Join collar by cast-on edge and sew to the base of neckband (ie picked up sts of neckband, do not join collar to top of neckband).

FINISHING OFF
Sew in sleeves, matching centre of each sleeve top with shoulder seam. Sew side and sleeve seams. Seams may be pressed using hot iron and damp cloth, but do not press ribs.

LONG MOHAIR WITH SHIRT COLLAR

*Easy

SIZE
To fit bust 87-92(92-98,98-104)cm [34-36(36-38,38-40)in]

MATERIALS
Yarn used in sample
Anne Rowena Mohair
Quantity
17(18,19) x 25g balls
Alternative yarn
Any mohair that knits up to same tension
Needles
1 pair each 4½mm (7) and 5½mm (5) needles
Buttons
3 x 25mm [1½in] domes

TENSION
Using 5½mm (5) needles over stocking stitch, 14 sts x 18/20 rows = 10 x 10cm [4 x 4in] (see Tension, page 11).

BACK
Rib With 4½mm needles, cast on 62(66,70) sts and work k1, p1 rib for 6cm [2½in].
Inc row Inc to 72(78,84) sts evenly over next row. Change to 5½mm needles. Work st st until work measures 39(42,45)cm [15½(16½,17¾)in] from beg.
Armhole shaping Cast off 8 sts at beg of next 2 rows*. Work straight for a further 30cm [12in].
Shoulder shaping Cast off 14(17,20) sts at beg of next 2 rows. Leave rem 28 sts on st holder/spare yrn.

FRONT
As for back to *
Neck opening Work further 5cm [2in]. K first 24(27,30) sts, turn. Work further 17cm [6½in] on these sts ending with a k row.
Neck shaping Cast off 4 sts at beg of next row, work 1 row. Cast off 3 sts at beg of next row. Work 1 row. Cast off 2 sts at beg of next row. Work 1 row. Cast off 1 st at beg of next row. Work straight until same length as back. Cast off all 14(17,20) sts. Leave centre 8 sts on safety pin and work other side to match, reversing shapings.

SLEEVES
Rib With 4½mm needles cast on 30 sts and work k1, p1 rib for 6cm [2½in].
Inc row Rib 2; (inc in next st) 26 times; rib to end [56 sts]. Change to 5½mm needles. Work st st.

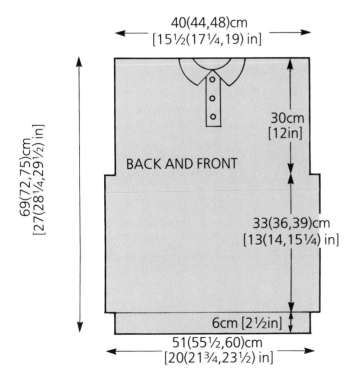

40(44,48)cm [15½(17¼,19) in]

30cm [12in]

BACK AND FRONT

33(36,39)cm [13(14,15¼) in]

69(72,75)cm [27(28¼,29½) in]

6cm [2½in]

51(55½,60)cm [20(21¾,23½) in]

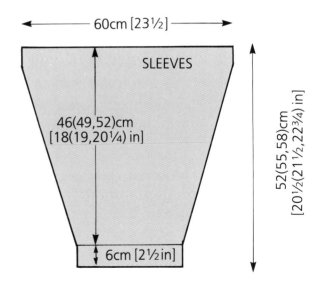

60cm [23½]

SLEEVES

46(49,52)cm [18(19,20¼) in]

52(55,58)cm [20½(21½,22¾) in]

6cm [2½in]

Sew sleeves in thus

Shaping Inc 1 st each end of 5th and every foll 4th row (ie 5th, 9th, 13th etc) to 86 sts. Work straight until sleeve measures 52(55,58)cm [20½(21½,22¾)in] from beg. Cast off loosely. (The sleeve top must fit in between the armhole shapings on front and back.)

COLLAR

Buttonband With 4½mm needles cast on 12 sts. Work k1, p1 rib until band, when slightly stretched, fits along left neck opening to start of neck shaping, ending with a rs row. Cast off 6 sts in rib; rib to end. Leave these 6 sts on safety pin. Sew band in place, sewing cast-on sts at base of opening behind the 8 sts on safety pin. Mark position of buttons with pin, the first 2cm [¾in] above lower edge, the last 1cm [½in] under top edge, rem one in between.

Buttonhole band Sl the 8 sts from safety pin onto 4½mm needles; (k1, p and k in next st, p1, k and p in next st) twice [12 sts]. Now work band in rib, making buttonholes to correspond with button placings.

Buttonhole (rs) Rib 3, yrn fwd, k2tog, rib to end. Work to measure same as buttonband when slightly stretched, ending with ws row. Cast off 6 sts ribwise. Leave rem 6 sts on safety pin. Sew band in position.

Collar Join shoulder seams, using backstitch so that no cast-off sts are visible. With rs facing and 4½mm needles, starting with the 6 sts on safety pin on buttonhole band, puk 25 sts up side, 28 sts across back and 25 sts down side, taking in 6 sts from safety pin [78 sts]. Work 10cm [4in] k1, p1 rib. Cast off loosely ribwise.

FINISHING OFF

Sew in sleeves, setting in cast-off edge square into armhole shaping. Sew side and sleeve seams. Sew buttons in place. Press seams with hot iron and damp cloth, but do not press ribs.

GEO

**Needs some experience

SIZE
To fit bust 87-92(92-98,98-104)cm [34-36(36-38,38-40)in]

MATERIALS
Yarn used in sample
Anne Rowena Mohair
Quantities
Main colour (navy) 14 x 25g balls (A)
1st contrast (gold) 2 x 25g balls (B)
2nd contrast (fuchsia) 3 x 25g balls (C)
3rd contrast (jade) 3 x 25g balls (D)
4th contrast (royal) 2 x 25g balls (E)
Alternative yarn
Any mohair that knits up to same tension
Needles
1 pair each 4½mm (7) and 5½mm (5) needles

TENSION
Using 5½mm (5) needles over stocking stitch, 14 sts x 18/20 rows = 10 x 10cm [4 x 4in] (see Tension, page 11).

BACK
Rib With 4½mm needles and A, cast on 56(62,68) sts and work k1, p1 rib for 10cm [4in].
Inc row Small: (inc in next st) twice; (rib 1, inc in next st) 26 times; (inc in next st) twice [86 sts]. Medium & Large: rib 1(4); (rib 1, inc in next st) 30 times, rib to end [92(98) sts]. Change to 5½mm needles.
Chart sequence for back and front
Rows 1-60: Work 43(46,49) sts of chart using 1st colourway, followed by 43(46,49) sts of chart using 2nd colourway.
Rows 61-62: Work 2 rows st st with C.
Rows 63 to end: Work 43(46,49) sts of chart with 3rd colourway, followed by 43(46,49) sts of chart using 4th colourway. If more rows are required, work 2 rows C, then start from row 1 again. Work until back measures 67(70,73)cm [26½(27½,28¾)in] from beg.
Shoulder shaping Cast off 8(9,10) sts at beg of next 2 rows, cast off 9(10,11) sts at beg of foll 4 rows. Leave rem 34 sts on st holder/spare yrn.

FRONT
As for back but work to 60(63,66)cm [23½(24¾,26)in] from beg.
Neck shaping Patt first 33(36,39) sts, turn and dec 1 st at beg of next and every foll alt row to 26(29,32) sts. Cont straight until front measures same as back.
Shoulder shaping Cast off 8(9,10) sts at beg of next row, work 1 row. Cast off 9(10,11) sts at beg of next and foll alt row. Thread centre 20 sts onto st holder and work rem 33(36,39) sts to match left side, reversing shapings.

SLEEVES
Rib With 4½mm needles and A, cast on 30 sts and work k1, p1 rib for 6cm [2½in].
Inc row Rib 3, (inc in next st, rib 1) 12 times; rib to end [42 sts]. Change to 5½mm needles.
Left sleeve Noting shaping, work 43 sts of chart (small size), bringing in 43rd st at first inc row. Work in 1st colourway. Leave extra sts plain A. When chart complete, work 2 rows st st with C. Complete sleeve by

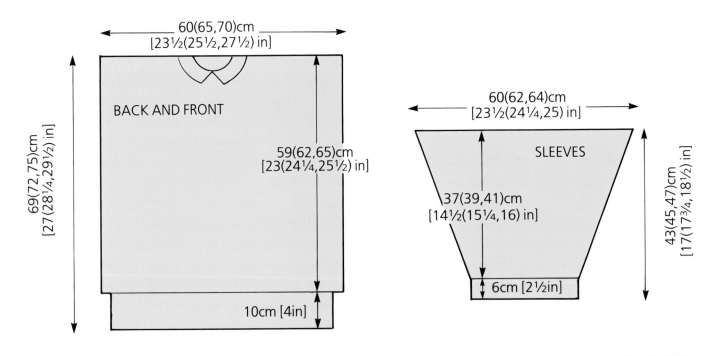

BACK AND FRONT

60(65,70)cm [23½(25½,27½) in]

69(72,75)cm [27(28¼,29½) in]

59(62,65)cm [23(24¼,25½) in]

10cm [4in]

SLEEVES

60(62,64)cm [23½(24¼,25) in]

37(39,41)cm [14½(15¼,16) in]

43(45,47)cm [17(17¾,18½) in]

6cm [2½in]

following chart working in 3rd colourway.

Right sleeve As for left, but work in 2nd colourway followed by 4th colourway.

Shaping Inc 1 st each end of 4th and every foll 3rd row (4th,7th,10th etc) until sleeve measures 43(45,47)cm [17(17¾,18½)in] from beg. Cast off loosely.

NECKBAND AND COLLAR

Join left shoulder using backstitch so that no cast-off sts are visible. With rs facing, using 4½mm needles and A, puk 34 sts from back, 14 sts down side, 20 sts from front and 14 sts up side [82 sts]. Work 4 rows k1, p1 rib. Cast off loosely, ribwise.

Collar With 4½mm needles and D, cast on 84 sts and work 10cm [4in] k1, p1 rib. Cast off loosely, ribwise. Join right shoulder, sew collar inside neckband, loosely, ensuring opening is at centre front of jumper. Join collar by cast-on edge and sew to base of neckband (ie picked-up sts of neckband, do not join collar to top of neckband).

FINISHING OFF

Sew in sleeves, matching centre of each sleeve top with shoulder seam. Sew side and sleeve seams. Seams may be pressed using hot iron and damp cloth, but do not press ribs.

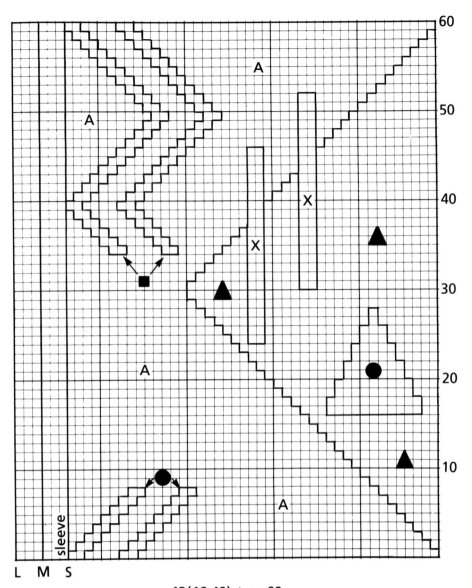

43(46,49)sts × 60 rows

KEY	1st	2nd	3rd	4th
□	A	A	A	A
▲	B	C	D	E
●	C	B	E	D
X	D	E	B	C
■	E	D	C	B

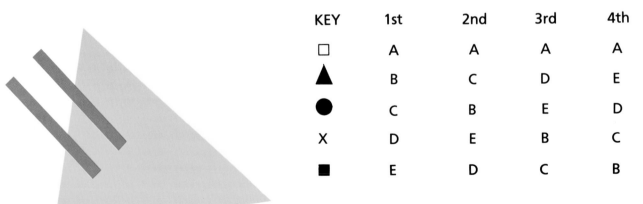

APRÈS SKI

*Easy

SIZE
To fit bust 87-92(92-98,98-104)cm [34-36(36-38,38-40)in]

MATERIALS
Yarn used in sample
Anne Rowena Mohair
Quantities
2-colourway version
Main colour (black) 12 x 25g balls (A)
1st contrast (white) 8 x 25g balls (B)

3-colourway version
Main colour (turquoise) 9 x 25g balls (A)
1st contrast (hot pink) 5 x 25g balls (B)
2nd contrast (citrus) 6 x 25g balls (C)
Alternative yarn
Any mohair that knits up to same tension
Needles
1 pair each 4½mm (7) and 5½mm (5) needles

TENSION
Using 5½mm (5) needles over stocking stitch, 14 sts x 18/20 rows = 10 x 10cm [4 x 4in] (see Tension, page 11).

Tip The back and front are mirror images of each other. Knit back first then, whilst working front reading the chart in opposite direction, lay the back down, wrong side up, so that you can see more clearly what front should look like as you knit it.

BACK
Rib With 4½mm needles and A, cast on 56(62,68) sts and work k1, p1 rib for 10cm [4in].
Inc row Small: (inc in next st) twice; (rib 1, inc in next st) 26 times; (inc in next st) twice [86 sts]. Medium & Large: rib 1(4); (rib 1, inc in next st) 30 times; rib to end [92(98) sts].
Change to 5½mm needles.
Now foll chart for back working in st st, noting beg and end sts for each size. Use separate balls of yrn for each block of colour to avoid drawing yrn across at back. Twist yrn round at back to prevent holes appearing. Work until back measures 67(70,73)cm [26½(27½,28¾)in] from beg.
Shoulder shaping Cast off 8(9,10) sts at beg of next 2 rows, cast off 9(10,11) sts at beg of foll 4 rows. Leave rem 34sts on st holder/spare yrn.

FRONT
As for back, working chart in mirror image, but working to 60(63,66)cm [23½(24¾,26)in] from beg.
Neck shaping
Patt first 33(36,39) sts, turn and dec 1 st at beg of next and every foll alt row to 26(29,32) sts. Cont straight until front measures same as back to shoulder shaping.
Shoulder shaping
Cast off 8(9,10) sts at beg of next row, work 1 row. Cast off 9(10,11) sts at beg of next and foll alt row. Thread centre 20 sts onto st holder and work rem 33(36,39) sts to match left side, reversing shapings.

SLEEVES
Rib With 4½mm needles and A, cast on 30 sts and work k1, p1 rib for 6cm [2½in].
Inc row Rib 3; (inc in next st, rib 1) 12 times; rib to end [42 sts]. Change to 5½mm needles and foll charts given for sleeves.

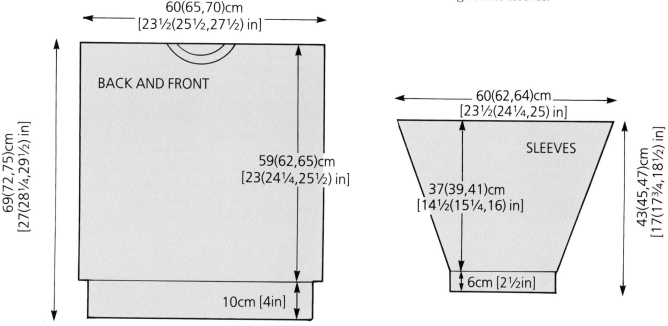

RIGHT SLEEVE ONLY

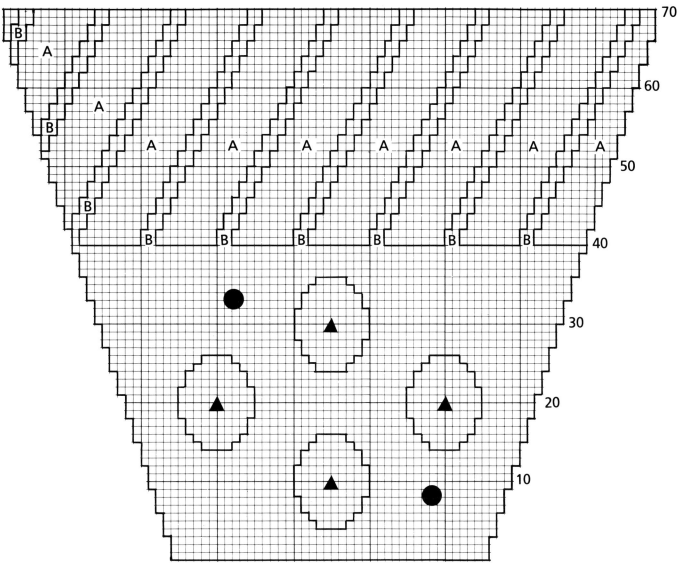

Shaping Inc 1 st each end of 4th and every foll 3rd row (4th, 7th, 10th etc) to end. When sleeve measures 43(45,47)cm [17(17¾,18½)in] from beg, cast off loosely.

NECKBAND
Join left shoulder using backstitch so that no cast-off sts are visible. With rs facing, using 4½mm needles and A, puk 34 sts from back, 14 sts down side, 20 sts from front, 14 sts up side [82 sts]. Work 8cm [3in] k1, p1 rib, cast off loosely, ribwise. Join right

shoulder and neckband seam. Fold neckband in half inwards and sew down inside.

FINISHING OFF
Sew in sleeves, matching centre of each sleeve top with shoulder seam. Sew side and sleeve seams. Seams may be pressed using hot iron and damp cloth, but do not press ribs.

KEY: A   B   ▲   ●   ✗
2 colourway version:- A   B   A   B   A
3 colourway version:- A   B   B   C   C

LEFT SLEEVE: Work rib & shaping as for right sleeve but work stripes as folls:-
8 rows A, 8 rows ●
8 rows A, 8 rows ●
etc. to end.

BACK AND FRONT

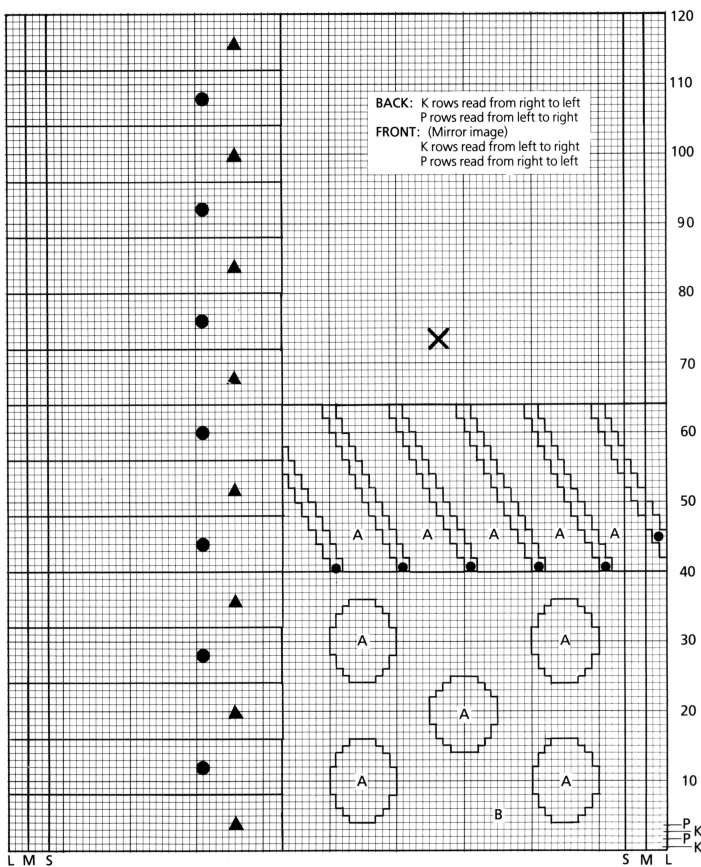

BACK: K rows read from right to left
P rows read from left to right
FRONT: (Mirror image)
K rows read from left to right
P rows read from right to left

ABSTRACTION

**Needs some experience

SIZE
To fit bust 87-92(92-98,98-104)cm
[34-36(36-38,38-40)in]

MATERIALS
Yarn used in sample
Anne Rowena Mohair
Quantities
Main colour (black) 11 x 25g balls (A)
1st contrast (royal) 4 x 25g balls (B)
2nd contrast (jade) 4 x 25g balls (C)
3rd contrast (fuchsia) 4 x 25g balls (D)
Alternative yarn
Any mohair that knits up to same
tension
Needles
1 pair each 4½mm (7) and 5½mm
(5) needles
Buttons
2 x triangular buttons

TENSION
Using 5½mm (5) needles over
stocking stitch, 14 sts x 18/20 rows =
10 x 10cm [4 x 4in] (see Tension,
page 11).

BACK
Rib With 4½mm needles and A, cast
on 70(76,82) sts and work k1, p1 rib
for 5cm [2in] ending with ws row.
Buttonhole Rib 6, cast off 3 sts, rib
to end of row. Next row: Rib to cast-
off sts, cast on 3 sts, rib 6. Cont to rib
until work measures 10cm [4in].
Front flap Cast off first 14 sts, rib to
end of row.
Inc row Small: (inc in next st) twice;
(rib 1, inc in next st) 26 times; (inc in
next st) twice [86 sts]. Medium &
Large: rib 1(4); (rib 1, inc in next st)
30 times; rib to end [92(98) sts].
Change to 5½mm needles.
Now foll chart for back working in st
st, noting beg and end sts for each
size. Use separate balls of yrn for
each block of colour to avoid drawing
yrn across at back. Twist yrn round at
back to prevent holes appearing.
Work until back measures
67(70,73)cm [26½(27½,28¾)in]
from beg.

Shoulder shaping
Shoulder shaping Cast off 8 (9,10)
sts at beg of next 2 rows, cast off
9(10,11) sts at beg of foll 4 rows.
Leave rem 34 sts on st holder/spare
yrn.

FRONT
Rib With 4½mm needles and A, cast
on 56(62,68) sts and work k1, p1 rib
for 10cm [4in].
Inc row As for back. Change to
5½mm needles. Foll chart for front
until work measures 60(63,66)cm
[23½(24¾,26)in] from beg.
Neck shaping Patt first 33(36,39)
sts, turn. Dec 1 st at beg of next and
every foll alt row to 26(29,32) sts.
Cont straight until front measures
same as back.
Shoulder shaping Cast off 8(9,10)
sts at beg of next row, work 1 row.
Cast off 9(10,11) sts at beg of next
and foll alt row. Thread centre 20 sts
onto st holder and work rem
33(36,39) sts to match left side,
reversing shapings.

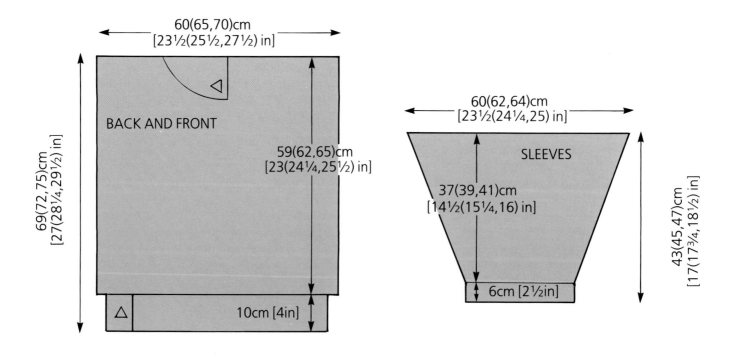

SLEEVES

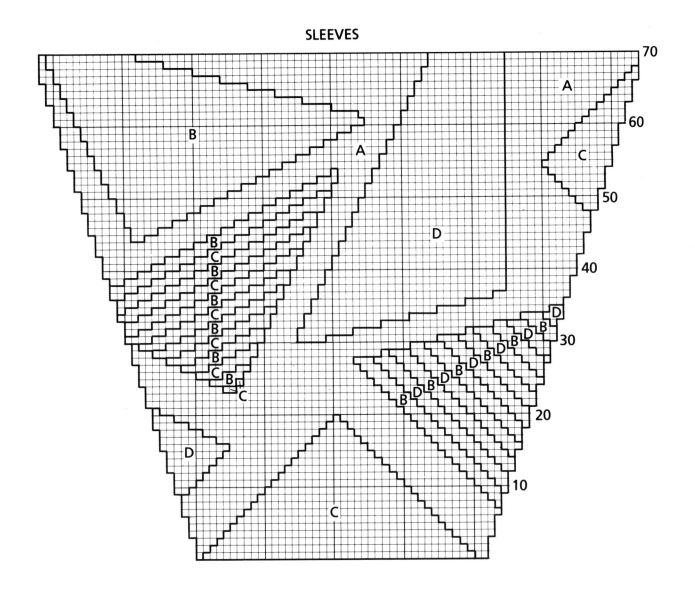

SLEEVES

Rib With 4½mm needles and A, cast on 30 sts and work k1, p1 rib for 6cm [2½in].

Inc row Rib 3, (inc in next st, rib 1) 12 times; rib to end [42 sts]. Change to 5½mm needles and foll charts given for sleeves.

Shaping Inc 1 st at each end of 4th and every foll 3rd row (4th, 7th, 10th etc) to end. When sleeve measures 43(45,47)cm [17(17¾,18½)in] from beg, cast off loosely.

COLLAR

Join right shoulder, using backstitch so that no cast-off sts are visible. With rs facing and using 4½mm needles and A, puk 14 sts down left side, 20 sts across front, 14 sts up right side and 34 sts from back [82 sts]. Work k1, p1 rib for 17 cm [6¾in], ending so that front, rs of jumper, is facing.

Buttonhole Rib 6, cast off 3 sts rib to end. Next row: Rib 73, cast on 3 sts, rib 6. Cont to rib normally until collar measures 20cm [8in]. Cast off ribwise.

FINISHING OFF

Join left shoulder using backstitch. Cont to sew 5cm [2in] of collar ensuring that seam is on inside when collar folds over shoulder. Sew in sleeves, using backstitch, matching centre of each sleeve top with shoulder seam. Sew side and sleeve seams. Seams may be pressed using hot iron and damp cloth, but do not press ribs. Sew on buttons to correspond with buttonholes.

BACK AND FRONT

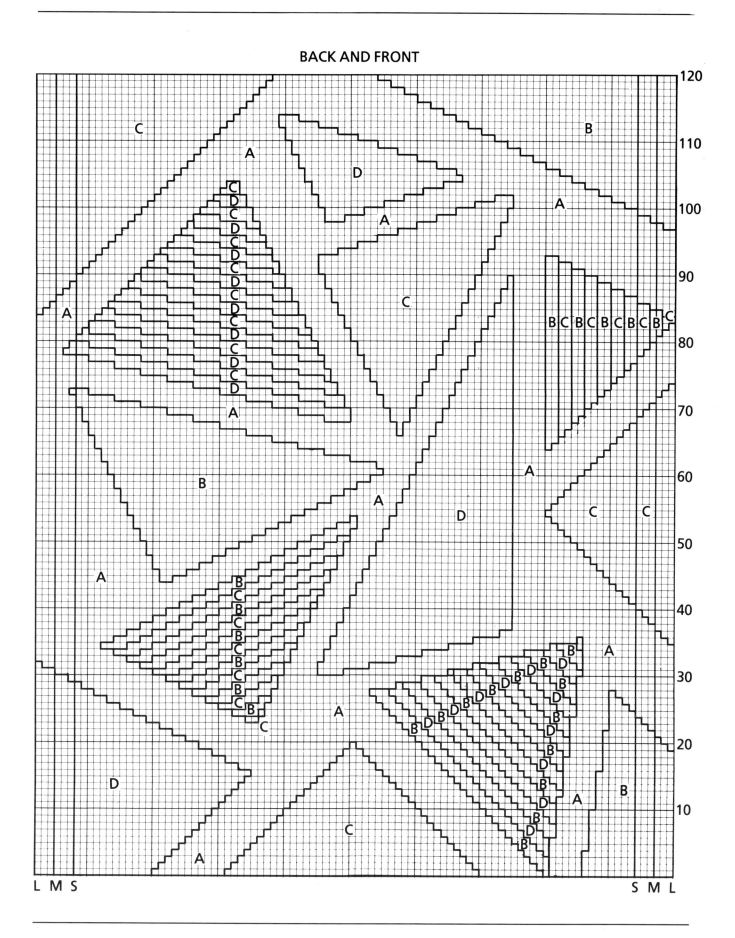

PAISLEY

**Needs some experience

SIZE
To fit bust 87-92(92-98,98-104)cm [34-36(36-38,38-40)in]

MATERIALS
Yarn used in sample
Anne Rowena Mohair
Quantities
Main colour (grey) 14 x 25g balls (A)
1st contrast (black) 4 x 25g balls (B)
2nd contrast (royal) 4 x 25g balls (C)
Alternative yarn
Any mohair that knits up to same tension
Needles
1 pair each 4½mm (7) and 5½mm (5) needles
Buttons
6 x 25mm [1in] domes

TENSION
Using 5½mm (5) needles over stocking stitch, 14 sts x 18/20 rows = 10 x 10cm [4 x 4in] (see Tension, page 11).

Tip The back and front are mirror images of each other. Knit back first then, whilst working the front reading the chart in opposite direction, lay the back down, wrong side up, so that you can see more clearly how front should look as you knit it.

BACK
Rib With 4½mm needles and A, cast on 70(76,82) sts and work 4 rows k1, p1 rib.
Buttonhole Rib 4, yrn fwd, k2tog, rib to end of row. Rib next row. Rep these 6 rows twice more.
Front flap Cast off first 14 sts, rib to end of row.
Inc row Small: (inc in next st) twice; (rib 1, inc in next st) 26 times; (inc in next st) twice [86 sts]. Medium & Large: rib 1(4); (rib 1, inc in next st) 30 times; rib to end [92(98) sts]. Change to 5½mm needles.
Foll chart for back, working in st st, noting beg and end sts for each size. Use separate balls of yrn for each block of colour to avoid drawing yrn across at back. Twist yrn around at back to prevent holes appearing.

Work until back measures 62(65,68)cm [24½(25½,26¾)in] from beg.
Shoulder shaping Cast off 11(12,13) sts at beg of next 6 rows. Leave rem 20 sts on st holder/spare yrn.

FRONT
Rib With 4½mm needles and A, cast on 56 (62,68) sts and work 19 rows k1, p1 rib.
Inc row As for back. Change to 5½mm needles. Foll chart for front until work measures 42(45,48)cm [16½(17¾,19)in].
Neck shaping Patt first 33(36,39) sts, turn. Cont on these sts only, keeping patt correct, until work measures 62(65,68)cm [24½(25½,26¾)in] from beg. Cast off 11(12,13) sts at beg of next and foll alt row. Thread centre 20 sts onto st holder. Work rem 33(36,39) sts to match left side, reversing shapings.

SLEEVES
Rib With 4½mm needles and A, cast on 30 sts and work k1, p1 rib for 6cm [2½in].

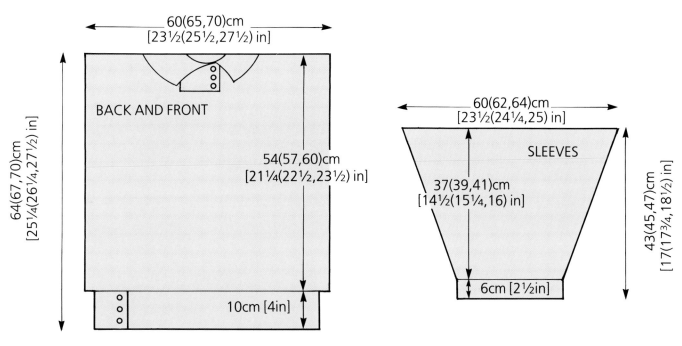

60(65,70)cm [23½(25½,27½) in]

BACK AND FRONT

64(67,70)cm [25¼(26¼,27½) in]

54(57,60)cm [21¼(22½,23½) in]

10cm [4in]

60(62,64)cm [23½(24¼,25) in]

SLEEVES

37(39,41)cm [14½(15¼,16) in]

43(45,47)cm [17(17¾,18½) in]

6cm [2½in]

RIGHT SLEEVE

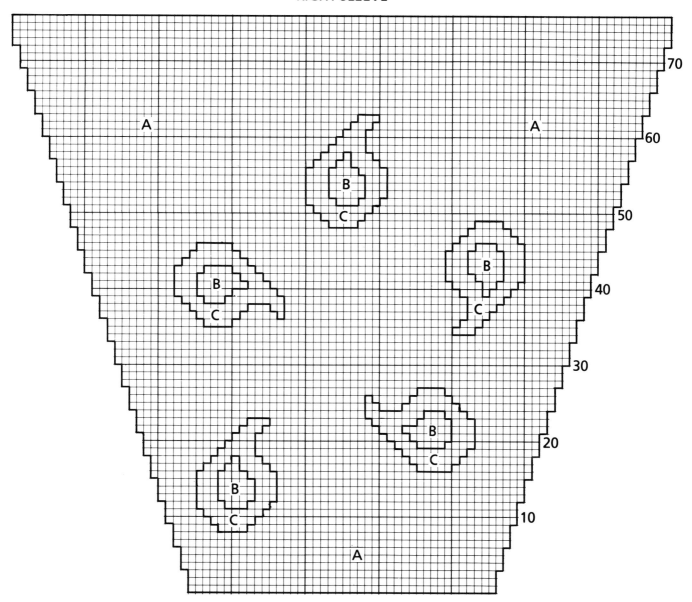

Inc row Rib 3; (inc in next st, rib 1) 12 times; rib to end [42 sts]. Change to 5½mm needles and foll charts given for sleeves.
Shaping Inc 1 st each end of 4th and every foll 3rd row (4th, 7th, 10th etc) to end. When sleeve measures 43(45,47)cm [17(17¾,18½)in] from beg, cast off loosely.

COLLAR
Join right shoulder, using backstitch so that no cast-off sts are visible. With ws of front facing, using 4½mm needles and A, pup 20 sts from st holder. Turn. Cast on 6 sts. K6; (k1, p1) to end. Next row: Rib to last 6 sts, p6. Rep these 2 rows twice more.
Buttonhole K2, yrn fwd, k2tog, k2, rib to end. Next row: rib to last 6 sts, p6. Rep last 6 rows twice more. Leave these sts on needle, sew side of this ribbed section to right-hand side of front only, leaving side with buttonholes free (see diagram – 1). Next row: cast off 6 sts, rib 20 sts. Now puk 20 sts up right side of front, 20 sts across back and cast on a further 40 sts. Rib across all 100 sts and cont until collar measures 15cm [6in] from back of neck. Cast off ribwise. Join left shoulder. Sew buttonhole band along bottom with a few securing sts (see diagram – 2). Join collar to left-hand side of front to halfway down, easing collar where

LEFT SLEEVE

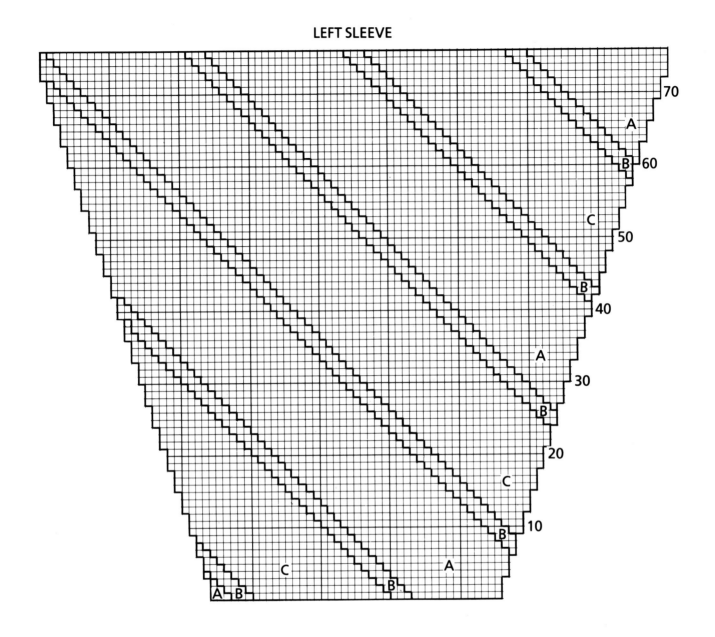

necessary and using a grafting st (see diagram – 3). Sew buttons onto front to correspond with buttonholes.

FINISHING OFF

Using backstitch, sew in sleeves, matching centre of each sleeve top with shoulder seam. Sew side and sleeve seams, leaving front flap free. Sew buttons onto front rib to correspond with buttonholes. Seams may be pressed using hot iron and damp cloth, but do not press ribs.

SEWING ON THE COLLAR

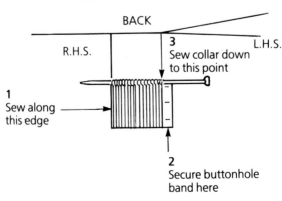

BACK

R.H.S.

3
Sew collar down
to this point

L.H.S.

1
Sew along
this edge

2
Secure buttonhole
band here

**Read BACK AND FRONT
chart opposite thus**

Back – K rows right to left
P rows left to right
Front – (Mirror image)
K rows left to right
P rows right to left

BACK AND FRONT

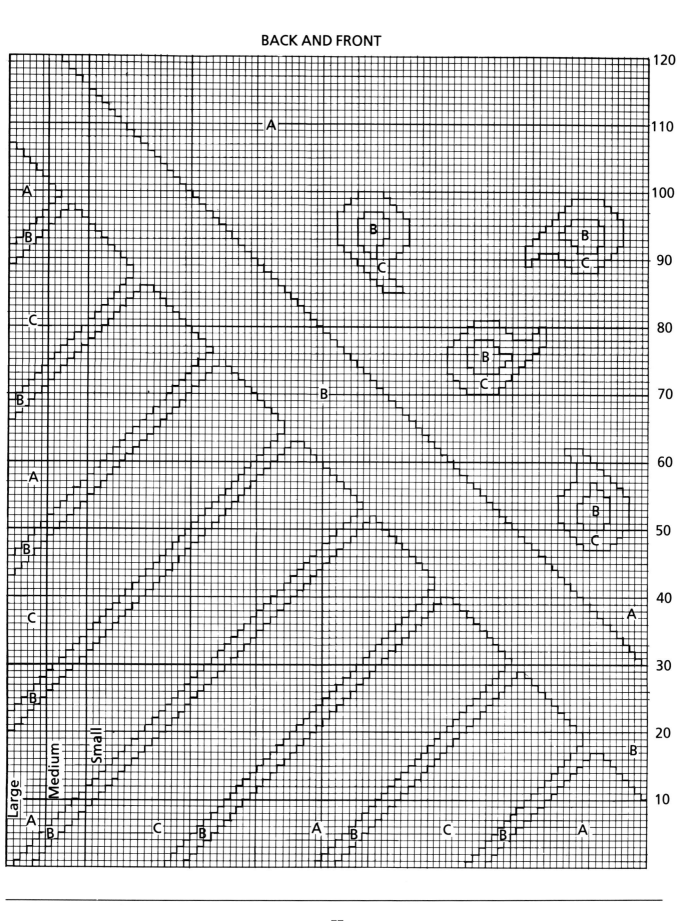

WOOL

Pure new wool has a unique combination of special qualities – warmth, softness and depth of colour. Wool may cost a little more sometimes, but its advantages make each purchase a real investment. Many people believe that wool is cold-weather wear and ignore it as a possible spring/summer choice. This is a misconception. Wool 'breathes', allowing air to flow between the fibres and between the skin and the garment. This quality enables wool to keep the wearer cool and fresh on all but the very hottest days.

Look for the Pure New Wool trade mark when choosing your yarn and you can look forward to knitting a garment that, with the correct care, will last a lifetime.

CERTIFICATION TRADE MARK
PURE NEW WOOL

SUMMER BORDER

**Needs some experience

SIZE
To fit bust 87-92(92-98,98-104)cm
[34-36(36-38,38-40)in]

MATERIALS
Yarn used in sample
Jaeger Matchmaker 2 DK
Quantities
Main colour (black 661) 16 x 50g
balls (A)
1st contrast (royal 672) 2 x 50g
balls (B)
2nd contrast (cherry 682) 1 x 50g
ball (C)
3rd contrast (mustard 685) 1 x 50g
ball (D)
4th contrast (emerald 669) 1 x 50g
ball (E)
Alternative yarn
Any DK yarn that knits up to same
tension
Needles
1 pair each 3¼mm (10) and 4mm
(8) needles
Buttons
8 x 14mm [½in] domes

TENSION
Using 4mm (8) needles over stocking
stitch, 24 sts x 32 rows = 10 x 10cm
[4 x 4in] (see Tension, page 11).

BACK
Rib With 3¼mm needles and A, cast
on 110(118,126) sts and work cable
rib as folls:
Rows 1,3 & 5: P2(3,3); *p1, k6, p1,
c6b&f (ie sl 2 sts onto cable needle
and hold at back of work, k1, k sts off
cable needle, sl 1 onto cable needle
and hold at front of work, k2, k st
from cable needle)*. Rep from * to *
7(8,8) times; p1(3,1); k6(0,6);
p3(0,4).
Row 2 and every alt row: K p sts and
p k sts.
Rows 7, 9 & 11: P2(3,3); *p1, c6b&f,
p1, k6* rep from * to * 7(8,8) times;
p1(3,1); 1st and 3rd sizes only c6b&f,
p3(0,4).
Row 12: As row 2.
These 12 rows form rib patt repeat.
When rib measures 10cm [4in] from
beg, with ws row facing, inc 18 sts

evenly over last row to 128(136,144)
sts. Change to 4mm needles and work
chart patts as folls:
Rows 1-52: Foll 52 rows of border
chart.
Rows 53-60: Work plain st st with A
(1 row k, 1 row p).
Rows 61-80: 14(18,22)A; (20 sts of
small chart, 20A) twice; 20 sts of
chart; 14(18,22)A.
Rows 81-90: Plain st st with A.
Rows 91-110: 14(18,22)A; (20A, 20
sts of chart) twice; 34(38,42)A.
Rows 111-120: Plain st st with A.
Rep from row 61 to end.
Work until back measures
62(65,68)cm [24¼(25½,26¾)in]
from beg.
Shoulder shaping Cast off
10(11,12) sts at beg of next 4 rows
and 11(12,13) sts at beg of foll 4
rows. Leave rem 44 sts on st holder/
spare yrn.

FRONTS
Pocket linings (2) With 4mm
needles and A, cast on 27 sts and

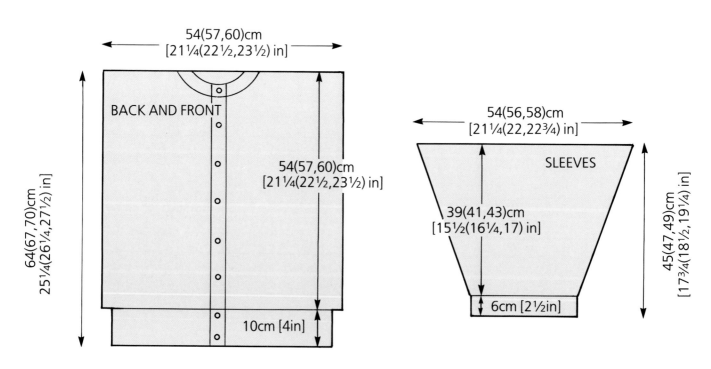

54(57,60)cm
[21¼(22½,23½) in]

BACK AND FRONT

54(57,60)cm
[21¼(22½,23½) in]

64(67,70)cm
25¼(26¼,27½) in]

10cm [4in]

54(56,58)cm
[21¼(22,22¾) in]

SLEEVES

39(41,43)cm
[15½(16¼,17) in]

45(47,49)cm
[17¾(18½,19¼) in]

6cm [2½in]

BORDER CHART

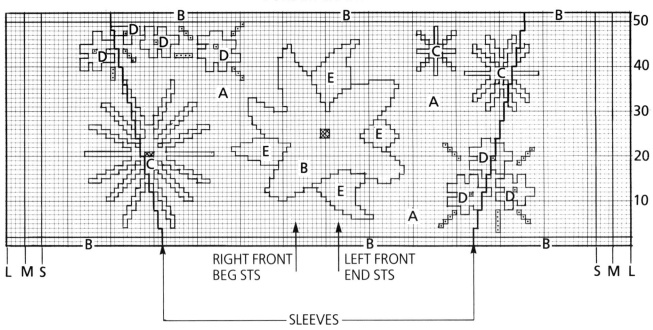

L M S   RIGHT FRONT BEG STS   LEFT FRONT END STS   **S M L**

SLEEVES

SMALL CHART

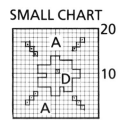

KEY

⊠ = D

· = E

work 12cm (4¾in) st st. Leave sts on st holder.

Left front With 3¼mm needles and A, cast on 52(56,60) sts. Work cable rib as folls:

Foundation row (rs) P1(0,2); *p1, k6, p1, c6b&f*, rep from * to * 3(4,4) times; p1(0,0); k6(0,0); p2(0,2). This row sets cable patt, work as for back, inc 7 sts evenly over last row to 59(63,67) sts. Work charts in the foll sequence, noting pocket placing:

Rows 1-60: As for back, but note end sts for left front.

Rows 61-80: 13(15,17)A; 20 sts of small chart; 26(28,30)A.

Rows 81-90: Plain st st with A.

Rows 91-110: 26(28,30)A; 20 sts of small chart; 13(15,17)A.

Rows 111-120: Plain st st with A.

Rep from row 61 to end.

Pocket placing Work patt for 12cm [4¾in]. Next row: k16(18,20) sts, sl next 27 sts onto st holder, k16(18,20). Next row: p16(18,20), p27 sts of pocket lining with ws facing, p16(18,20). Cont with patt until work measures 56(59,62)cm [22(23¼,24½)in] from beg ending with k row.

Neck shaping With ws facing, sl first 8 sts onto safety pin, patt to end of row. Dec 1 st at neck edge every row to 42(46,50) sts. Work to measure same length as back.

Shoulder shaping Cast off 10(11,12) sts at beg of next and foll alt row, work 1 row. Cast off 11(12,13) sts at beg of next and foll alt row.

Right front Work as for left, including pocket placings, but reverse neck shaping. Pocket placing is the same as for left front.

SLEEVES

Rib With 3¼mm needles and A, cast on 58 sts and work cable rib as folls:

Foundation row (rs) P1 *p1, k6, p1, c6b&f*. Rep from * to * 4 times, p1. Work rib as for back on sts as set. Work 11 rows only.

Inc row Working in patt, inc 14 sts evenly over last row – (work 3, inc in next st) 14 times, work to end of row [72 sts]. Change to 4mm needles and work chart in foll sequence, noting sleeve shaping at the same time:

Chart sequence

Rows 1-60: As for back, noting beg and end sts for sleeve.

Rows 61-80: Plain A to centre 80 sts, (20 sts from small chart, 20A) twice, plain A to end.

Rows 81-90: Plain st st with A.

Rows 91-110: Plain A to centre 80 sts, (20A, 20 sts from chart) twice, plain A to end.

Rows 111-120: Plain st st with A.

Rep from row 61 to end.

Sleeve shaping Inc 1 st each end of 5th and every foll 4th row to end, until sleeve measures 45(47,49)cm [17¾(18½,19¼)in] from beg. Cast off loosely.

FRONT BANDS

Buttonband (left side) With 3¼mm needles and A, cast on 11 sts and work k1, p1, rib until band measures from beg of rib to beg of neck shaping when slightly stretched. With ws facing, cast off 6 sts, leave rem 5 sts on pin. Place seven buttons evenly spaced along band, graft band in place.

Buttonhole band (right side) As for buttonband but make buttonholes to correspond with button placings.

Buttonhole Rib 5, yrn fwd, k2tog, rib to end. Rib next row. Graft band in place.

Neckband Join both shoulders using backstitch so that no cast-off sts are visible. With rs facing, using 3¼mm needles and A, starting with buttonhole band, puk 5 sts from safety pin then 8 sts from right front, 28 sts up side, 44 sts from back, 28 sts down side, 8 sts from left front and 5 sts from buttonband safety pin [126 sts]. Work 6cm [2½in] k1, p1 rib making two more buttonholes at 2cm [¾in] and 4cm [1½in] on buttonhole side of neckband. Cast off loosely, ribwise. Fold band in half inwards and sew down, making sure the buttonholes fall over each other. Sew on rem button to correspond with buttonhole.

FINISHING OFF

Pocket tops With 3¼mm needles and A, puk 27 sts from st holder and work 6 rows k1, p1 rib. Cast off ribwise, loosely. Sew pocket linings to inside of cardigan fronts and neatly sew down pocket tops to outside. Press each piece separately before sewing up, using hot iron and damp cloth. Sew in sleeves, matching centre of each sleeve top to shoulder seam. Sew side and sleeve seams, press seams. If cable rib curls up slightly, press very gently with damp cloth.

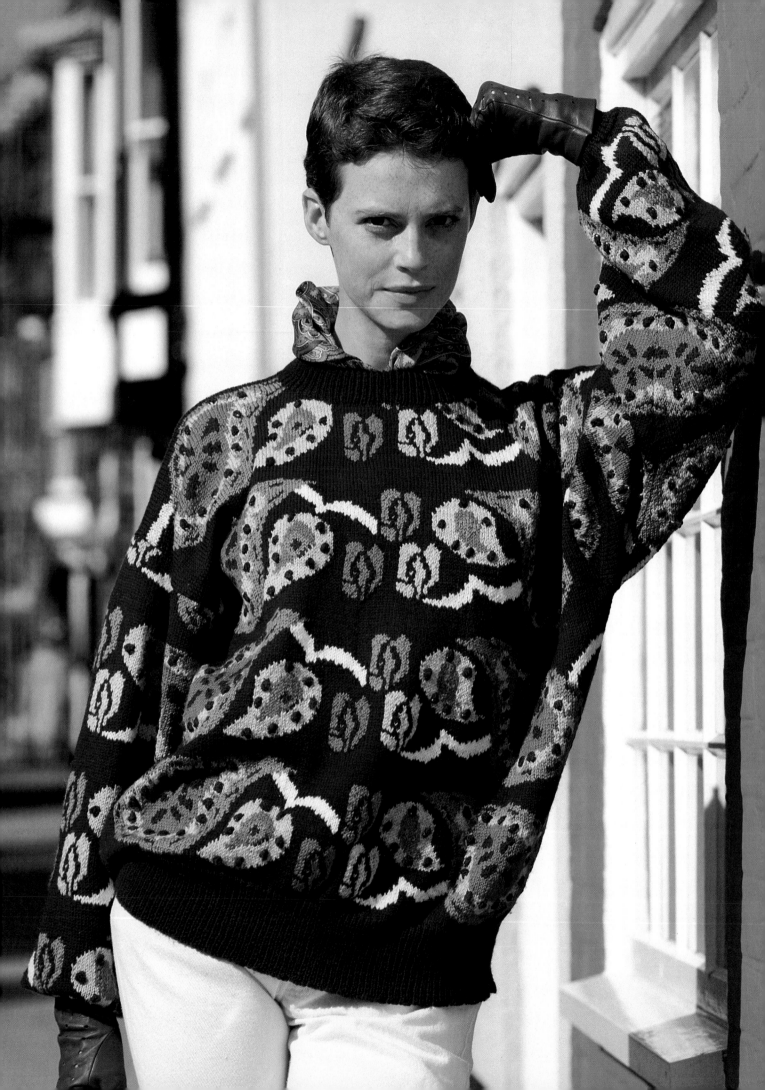

ALL OVER PAISLEY

***Difficult

SIZE
To fit bust 87-92(92-98,98-104)cm [34-36(36-38,38-40)in]

MATERIALS
Yarn used in sample
Jaeger Merino 4 ply
Quantities
Main colour (navy 674) 8 x 50g balls (A)
1st contrast (cream 662) 1 x 50g ball (B)
2nd contrast (stone 728) 2 x 50g balls (C)
3rd contrast (oatmeal 693) 2 x 50g balls (D)
4th contrast (olive 731) 2 x 50g balls (E)
Alternative yarn
Any 4 ply yarn that knits up to same tension
Needles
1 pair each 3mm (11) and 3¼mm (10) needles

TENSION
Using 3¼mm (10) needles over stocking stitch, 30 sts x 40 rows = 10 x 10cm [4 x 4in] (see Tension, page 11).

BACK
Rib With 3mm needles and A, cast on 158(166,174) sts and work k1, p1 rib for 8cm [3¼in], inc 20 sts evenly over last row to 178(186,194) sts. Change to 3¼mm needles and foll chart as given for back, rep the 50 rows of chart to end. When work measures 37(39,41)cm [14½(15¼,16)in], shape for armhole.
Armhole shaping K2tog at each end of next and foll alt row. P next row. K2tog each end of next and every 4th row to 166(174,182) sts*. Cont straight until armhole measures 26cm [10¼in] from beg of shaping.
Shoulder shaping Cast off 13(14,15) sts at beg of next 6 rows, 14(15,16) sts at beg of foll 2 rows, leaving rem 60 sts on st holder/spare yrn.

FRONT
As for back to *. Cont straight until armhole measures 19cm [7½in] from beg of shaping.
Neck shaping Patt first 67(71,75) sts, turn. Dec 1 st at neck edge on next and every row to 53(57,61) sts. Work to measure same length as back.
Shoulder shaping Cast off 13(14,15) sts at beg of next and foll alt 2 rows, work 1 row. Cast off rem 14(15,16) sts. Leave centre 32 sts on st holder and work rem sts to match left side, reversing shapings.

SLEEVES
Rib With 3mm needles and A, cast on 62 sts. Work 6cm [2in] k1, p1 rib, inc 30 sts evenly over last row to 92 sts. Change to 3¼mm needles and foll chart as shown for sleeves, at the same time inc 1 st each end of 5th and every foll 4th row to 164 sts. Work straight until sleeve measures 45(47,49)cm [17¾(18½,19¼)in] from beg.

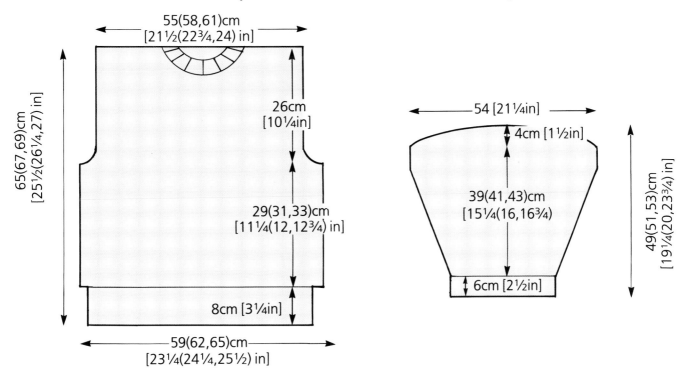

BACK, FRONT AND SLEEVES

These 50 rows form pattern and are repeated

SLEEVES

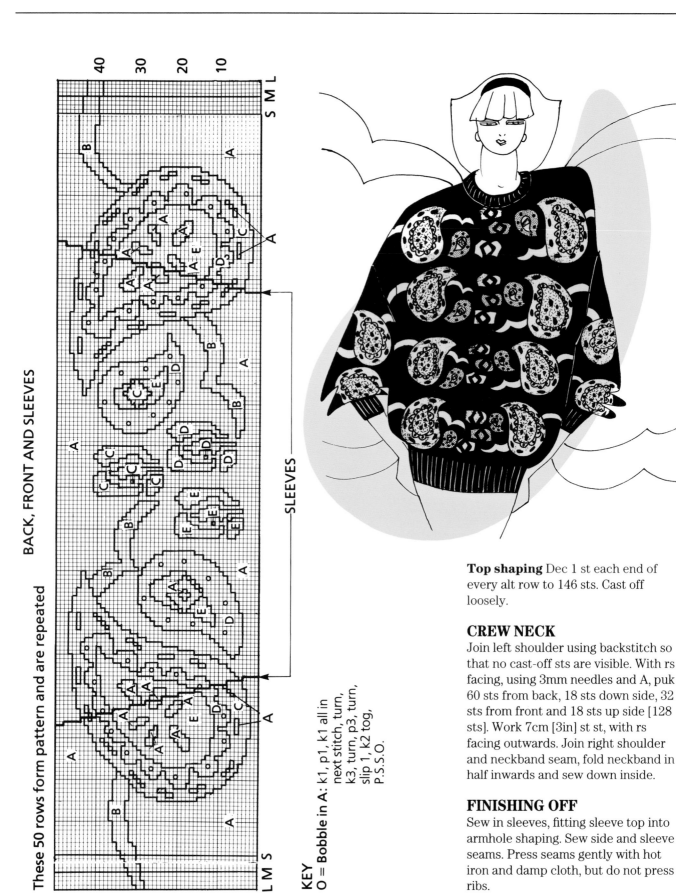

KEY
O = **Bobble in A:** k1, p1, k1 all in next stitch, turn, k3, turn, p3, turn, slip 1, k2 tog, P.S.S.O.

Top shaping Dec 1 st each end of every alt row to 146 sts. Cast off loosely.

CREW NECK

Join left shoulder using backstitch so that no cast-off sts are visible. With rs facing, using 3mm needles and A, puk 60 sts from back, 18 sts down side, 32 sts from front and 18 sts up side [128 sts]. Work 7cm [3in] st st, with rs facing outwards. Join right shoulder and neckband seam, fold neckband in half inwards and sew down inside.

FINISHING OFF

Sew in sleeves, fitting sleeve top into armhole shaping. Sew side and sleeve seams. Press seams gently with hot iron and damp cloth, but do not press ribs.

FESTIVAL

**Needs some experience

SIZE
To fit bust 87-92(92-98,98-104)cm [34-36(36-38,38-40)in]

MATERIALS
Yarn used in sample
Anne Rowena DK
Quantities
Main colour (navy) 8 x 50g balls (A)
1st contrast (jade) 2 x 50g balls (B)
2nd contrast (gold) 1 x 50g ball (C)
3rd contrast (blue) 2 x 50g balls (D)
4th contrast (fuchsia) 2 x 50g balls (E)
Alternative yarn
Any DK that knits up to same tension
Needles
1 pair each 3¼mm (10) and 4½mm (7) needles

TENSION
Using 4½mm (7) needles over stocking stitch, 22 sts x 28 rows = 10 x 10cm [4 x 4in] (see Tension, page 11).

BACK
Rib With 3¼mm needles and A, cast on 98(106,114) sts and work k1, p1 rib for 10cm [4in].
Inc row Inc 20 sts evenly over last row to 118(126,134) sts. Change to 4½mm needles and foll chart patt in foll sequence:
Rows 1-88: Foll chart working in 1st colourway.
Rows 89-176: Foll chart working in 2nd colourway.
Work to 67(70,73)cm [26¼(27½,28¾)in] from beg.
Shoulder shaping Cast off 9(10,11) sts at beg of next 4 rows, then cast off 8(9,10) sts at beg of foll 4 rows. Leave rem 50 sts on st holder/spare yrn.

FRONT
Work as for back to 60(63,66)cm [23½(24¾,26)in] from beg.
Neck shaping Patt first 44(48,52) sts, turn, dec 1 st at neck edge next and every alt row to 34(38,42) sts,

ending with p row.
Shoulder shaping Cast off 9(10,11) sts at beg of next and foll alt row. Work 1 row. Cast off 8(9,10) sts at beg of next and foll alt row. Leave centre 30 sts on st holder and work rem sts to match left side, reversing shapings.

SLEEVES
Rib With 3¼mm needles and A, cast on 48 sts and work 6cm [2½in] k1, p1 rib.
Inc row Rib 6; (rib 1, inc in next st) 18 times; rib to end [66 sts]. Change to 4½mm needles and foll chart as shown for sleeves in the same colourway sequence as given for back, at the same time inc 1 st at each end of 5th and every foll 4th row to end. When sleeve measures 45(47,49)cm [17¾(18½,19¼)in] from beg, cast off loosely.

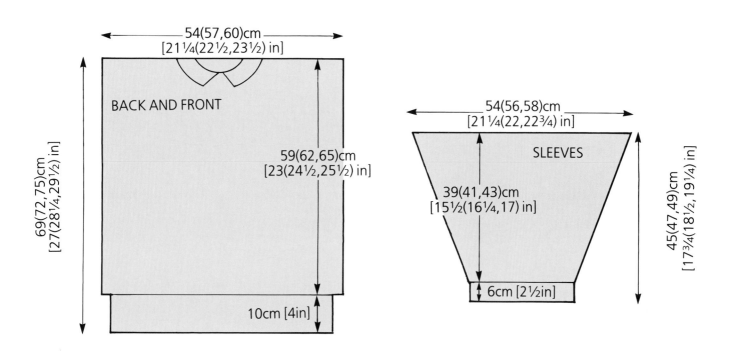

BACK AND FRONT

54(57,60)cm [21¼(22½,23½) in]

69(72,75)cm [27(28¼,29½) in]

59(62,65)cm [23(24½,25½) in]

10cm [4in]

SLEEVES

54(56,58)cm [21¼(22,22¾) in]

39(41,43)cm [15½(16¼,17) in]

45(47,49)cm [17¾(18½,19¼) in]

6cm [2½in]

BACK, FRONT AND SLEEVES

These 88 rows form pattern and are repeated using second colourway.

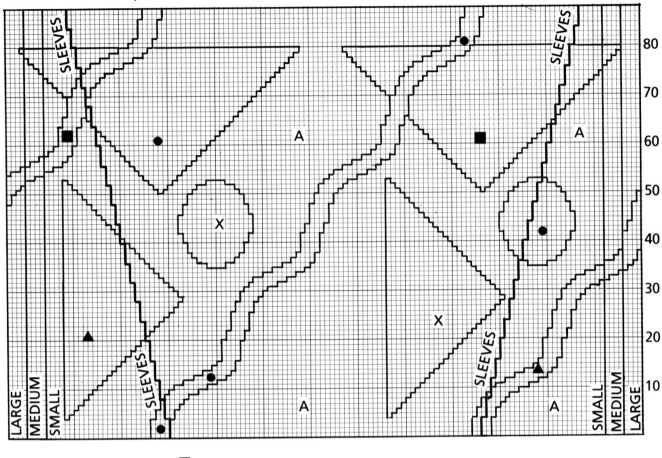

KEY =   ▲   X   ●   ■

	1st	B	C	D	E
	2nd	D	B	E	C

COLLAR

Join left shoulder using backstitch so that no cast-off sts are visible. With rs facing, using 3¼mm needles and A, puk 50 sts from back, 20 sts down left side, 30 sts from front, 20 sts up right side [120 sts]. Work 2cm [¾in] k1, p1 rib, cast off loosely, ribwise. With 3¼mm needles and B, cast on 122 sts and work k1, p1 rib for 8 cm [3¼in]. Cast off loosely, ribwise. Join right shoulder and neckband and sew collar inside neckband making sure opening of collar falls exactly in centre front and that neckband is free (ie join collar to base of neckband rows).

FINISHING OFF

Press each piece separately using hot iron and damp cloth. Sew in sleeves matching centre of each sleeve top with shoulder seam. Sew side and sleeve seams. Press seams, but do not press ribs.

DIAMONDS

***Difficult

SIZE
To fit bust 87-92(92-98,98-104)cm
[34-36(36-38,38-40)in]

MATERIALS
Yarn used in sample
Rowan Lightweight DK
Quantities
Main colour (natural 84) 17 x 25g
hanks (A)
Trellis: (taupe 616) 3 x 25g hanks (B)
(brown 98) 3 x 25g hanks (C)
Leaves: (dk green 606) 2 x 25g hanks
(D) (green 73) 1 x 25g
hank (E)
Flowers: (red 45) 1 x 25g hank (F)
(coral 66) 1 x 25g hank G)
(yellow 12) 1 x 25g hank (H)
(lemon 116) 1 x 25g hank (I)
(dk blue 108) 1 x 25g hank (J)
(lt blue 55) 1 x 25g hank (K)
(purple 94) 1 x 25g hank (L)
(lilac 128) 1 x 25g hank (M)
Alternative yarn
Any DK that knits up to same tension
Needles
1 pair each 3¼mm (10) and 4mm
(8) needles

1 cable needle for ribs
1 circular needle 3¼mm (10) for
collar

TENSION
Using 4mm (8) needles over stocking
stitch, 24 sts x 32 rows = 10 x 10cm
[4 x 4in] (see Tension, page 11).

Tip You will be using many different
colours all at once with this design.
Read notes on Working with Many
Colours first. For best results use
lengths of yarn for each new colour
but take background colour across at
back of work *except* in particularly
large areas of contrast colour, eg
some of the petals span several
stitches; in those cases join in a new
ball of background colour too.

BACK
Rib With 3¼mm needles and A, cast
on 99(107,115) sts and work rib as
folls:
Row 1: *P1; (k1, p1) 4(6,8) times*;
[k1, p1, c2b, k1, c2f, p1, k1; (k1, p1) 7
times; p1] 4 times, but ending (p1,
k1) 4(6,8) times; p1 on last rep.

Row 2: *K1; (p1, k1) 4(6,8) times*;
[p1, k1, p5, k1, p1; (k1, p1) 7 times;
k1] 4 times, ending (k1, p1) 4(6,8)
times; k1 on last rep.
Row 3: As row 1 * to *; [k1, c2b, k3,
c2f, k1; (p1, k1) 7 times; p1] 4 times,
ending as row 1.
Row 4: As row 2 * to *; [p9; (k1, p1) 7
times; k1] 4 times, ending as row 2.
Row 5: As row 1 * to *; [c2b, k5, c2f;
(p1, k1) 7 times; p1] 4 times etc.
Row 6: As row 4.
Row 7: As row 1 * to *; [k9; (p1, k1) 7
times; p1] 4 times etc.
Row 8: As row 4.
Row 9: As row 1 * to *; [c2f, k5, c2b;
(p1, k1) 7 times; p1] 4 times etc.
Row 10: As row 4.
Row 11: As row 1 * to *; [k1, c2f, k3,
c2b, k1; (p1, k1) 7 times; p1] 4 times
etc.
Row 12: As row 2.
Row 13: As row 1 * to *; [k1, p1, c2f,
k1, c2b, p1, k1; (p1, k1) 7 times; p1] 4
times etc.
Row 14: As row 2.
Row 15: As row 1 * to *; [k1, p1, k1,
c3f, k1, p1, k1; (p1, k1) 7 times; p1] 4
times etc.

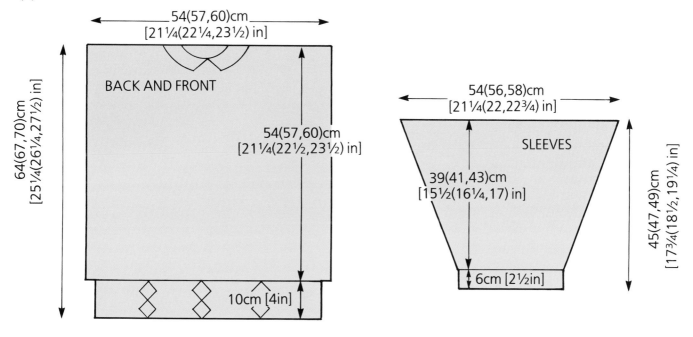

Row 16: As row 2.
These 16 rows form rib patt. Rep them once more, inc extra sts on last row thus:
Inc row Rib 5(11,17); (inc in next st, rib 2) 29 times; rib to end [128(136,144) sts]. Change to 4mm needles and foll chart as given. Work to 62(65,68)cm [24¼(25½,26¾)in] from beg.
Shoulder shaping Cast off 10(11,12) sts at beg of next 4 rows,

and 11(12,13) sts at beg of foll 4 rows. Leave rem 44 sts on st holder/spare yrn.

FRONT
As for back until work measures 55(58,61)cm [21½(22¾,24)in] from beg.
Neck shaping Patt first 51(55,59) sts, turn. Dec 1 st at neck edge next and every alt row to 42(46,50) sts, ending with a p row. Work to

62(65,68)cm [24¼(25½,26¾)in] from beg.
Shoulder shaping Cast off 10(11,12) sts at beg of next and foll alt row, work 1 row. Cast off 11(12,13) sts at beg of next and foll alt row. Sl centre 26 sts onto safety pin and work rem sts to match left side, reversing shapings.

SLEEVES
Rib With 3¼mm needles and A, cast on 49 sts and work rib as for back starting thus:
Row 1: (K1, p1) 4 times; [k1, p1, c2b, k1, c2f, p1, k1; (p1, k1) 7 times; p1] twice, ending (p1, k1) 4 times. Now work as given for back on sts as set. Work 15 rows.
Inc row Work as row 16 but inc extra sts as folls: rib 1; (rib 1, inc in next st) 23 times; rib to end [72 sts]. Change to 4mm needles and foll chart for sleeves, at the same time inc 1 st each end of 5th and every foll 4th row to end until sleeve measures 45(47,49)cm [17(17¾, 18½)in] from beg. Cast off loosely.

COLLAR
Join both shoulders using backstitch so that no cast-off sts are visible. With 3¼mm circular needle, starting in centre of front, puk 13 sts from front, 25 sts up side, 44 sts from back, 25 sts down side and 13 sts from front. Mark end of row with contrast yrn. Work 6 rows k1, p1 rib in rounds, ending above marked st. Now work in rows, thus dividing for collar. Cont in k1, p1 rib for a further 8cm [3¼in]. Cast off neatly, ribwise.

FINISHING OFF
Press all pieces using hot iron and damp cloth before joining together. Sew in sleeves matching centre of each sleeve top with shoulder seam. Press these seams. Sew side and sleeve seams, using backstitch or invisible grafting st. Press rem seams, but do not press ribs.

SLEEVES

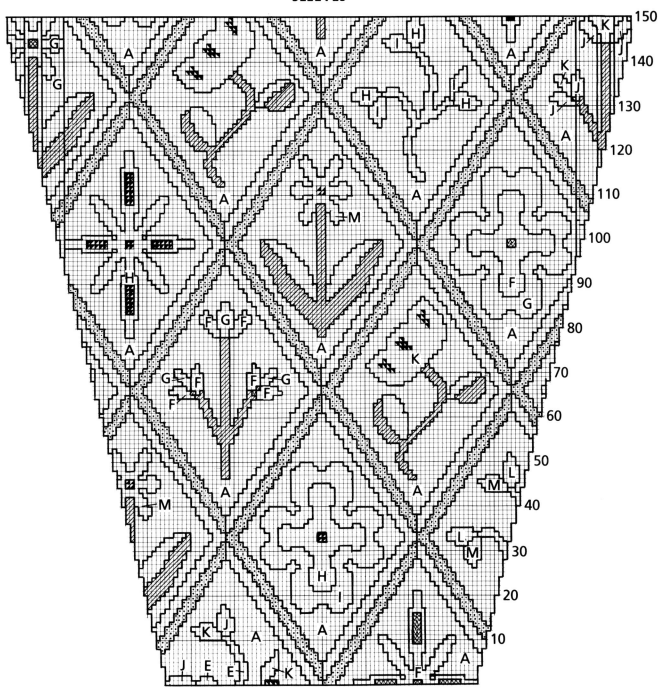

KEY

Diamond Trellis	☐ = **B**;	⊡ = **C**
Leaves and Stems	☐ = **E**;	◩ = **D**
flowers	⊠ = **F**;	▽ = **G**; ⊙ = **H**; ◪ = **I**;
	◣ = **J**;	◣ = **K**; ◪ = **L**; ■ = **M**

NB Work charts in st st – weave in background colour, but use separate balls, or lengths, for each new colour section.

BACK AND FRONT

BLOOMS

**Needs some experience

SIZE
To fit bust 87-92(92-98,98-104)cm
[34-36(36-38,38-40)in]

MATERIALS
Yarn used in sample
Anne Rowena DK
Quantities
Main colour (black) 6 x 50g (A)
1st contrast (grey) 3 x 50g (B)
2nd contrast (ecru) 4 x 50g (C)
Alternative yarn
Any DK that knits up to same tension
Needles
1 pair each 3¼mm (10) and 4mm
(8) needles

TENSION
Using 4mm (8) needles over stocking
stitch, 24sts x 32 rows = 10 x 10cm
[4 x 4in] (see Tension, page 11).

BACK
Rib With 3¼mm needles and A, cast
on 98(106,114) sts and work k1, p1
rib for 10cm [4in].

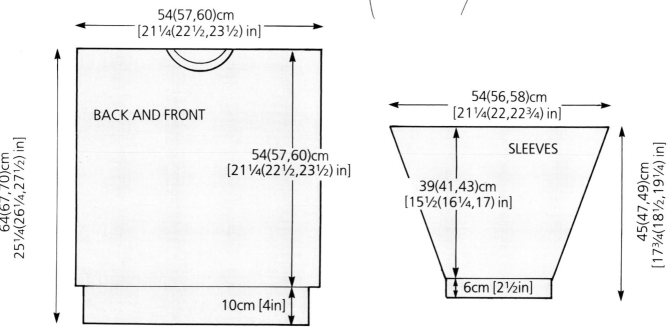

54(57,60)cm
[21¼(22½,23½) in]

BACK AND FRONT

54(57,60)cm
[21¼(22½,23½) in]

64(67,70)cm
25¼(26¼,27½) in]

10cm [4in]

54(56,58)cm
[21¼(22,22¾) in]

SLEEVES

39(41,43)cm
[15½(16¼,17) in]

45(47,49)cm
[17¾(18½,19¼) in]

6cm [2½in]

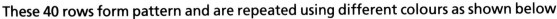

These 40 rows form pattern and are repeated using different colours as shown below

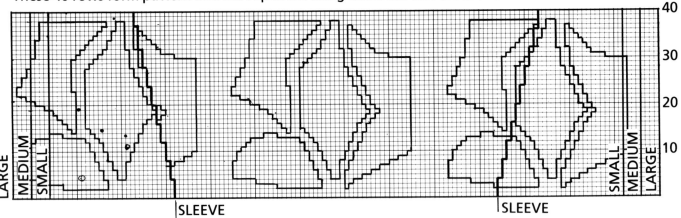

SLEEVE

SLEEVE

COLOUR SEQUENCES:
1st Repeat:- Background = B, Flowers = A.
2nd Repeat:- Background = C, Flowers = B.
3rd Repeat:- Background = A, Flowers = C.
NOW REPEAT FROM BEGINNING

Inc row Rib 4(8,12) sts; (inc in next st, rib 2) 30 times; rib to end [128(136,144) sts]. Change to 4mm needles and foll chart as given noting colours to be used. Rep the 40 rows of chart until work measures 62(65,68)cm [24¼(25½,26¾)in] from beg.
Shoulder shaping Cast off 10(11,12) sts at beg of next 4 rows and 11(12,13) sts at beg of foll 4 rows. Leave rem 44 sts on st holder/ spare yrn.

FRONT
As for back but work to 55(58,61)cm [21½(23,24)in] from beg.
Neck shaping Patt first 51(55,59) sts, turn. Dec 1 st at neck edge next and every alt row to 42(46,50) sts, ending with p row. Work straight to match back length.
Shoulder shaping Cast off 10(11,12) sts at beg of next and foll alt row, work 1 row. Cast off 11(12,13) sts at beg of next and foll alt row. Leave centre 26 sts on st holder and work rem sts to match left side, reversing all shapings.

SLEEVES
Rib With 3¼mm needles and A, cast on 48 sts and work 6cm [2½in] k1, p1 rib.
Inc row (Rib 1, inc in next st) to end [72 sts]. Change to 4mm needles and foll chart as given for sleeves, at the same time inc 1 st each end of 5th and every foll 4th row until sleeves measure 45(47,49)cm [17¾(18½,19¼)in] from beg. Cast off loosely.

CREW NECK
Join left shoulder using backstitch so that no cast-off sts are visible. With rs facing, using 3¼mm needles and A, puk 44 sts from back, 28 sts down left side, 26 sts from front and 28 sts up right side [126sts]. Work 6cm [2½in] k1, p1 rib, cast off loosely, ribwise. Join right shoulder and neckband seam. Fold collar in half inwards and sew down – secure, but not too tight.

FINISHING OFF
Press each piece separately before sewing up, using hot iron and damp cloth. Sew in sleeves matching centre of each sleeve top to shoulder seam, press seams. Sew side and sleeve seams, press seams, but do not press ribs.

AEROBICS

**Needs some experience

SIZE
To fit bust 87-92(92-98,98-104)cm
[34-36(36-38,38-40)in]

MATERIALS
Yarn used in sample
Jaeger Sport
Quantities
Main colour (cream 220) 8 x 50g (A)
1st contrast (black 216) 7 x 50g (B)
2nd contrast (pillar box 237)
7 x 50g (C)
Alternative yarn
Any Sport or Aran type yarn that
knits up to same tension
Needles
1 pair each 4½mm (7) and 5mm (6)
needles

TENSION
Using 5mm (6) needles over stocking
stitch, 17/18 sts x 25/26 rows =
10 x 10cm [4 x 4in] (see Tension,
page 11).

BACK
Rib With 4½mm needles and B, cast
on 68(74,80) sts; then work k2, p2 rib
as folls:
Row 1: K2A, p2A (0; k2A, p2A); *k2B
(using manageable lengths or small
balls), p2A, k2A, p2A, k2A, p2A*, rep
from * to * 5(6,6) times; k2B, p2A
(k2B; k2B, p2A).
Row 2: Work to match row 1, p B sts.
Work 8cm [3¼in] ending with rs row.
Inc row P4(7,10); (p1, inc in next st)
30 times; p to end [98(104,110) sts].
Change to 5mm needles. Now foll
chart as given, noting beg and end sts
for each size. Work until back
measures 67(70,73)cm
[26¼(27½,28¾)in] from beg.
Shoulder shaping Cast off
10(11,12) sts at beg of next 2 rows.
Cast off 11(12,13) sts at beg of foll 4
rows. Leave rem 34 sts on st holder/
spare yrn.

FRONT
As for back but work to 60(63,66)cm
[23½(24¾,26)in] from beg.

Neck shaping Patt first 39(42,45)
sts, turn and dec 1 st at beg of next
row and every foll alt row to 32
(35,38) sts. Cont straight until front
measures same as back.
Shoulder shaping Cast off
10(11,12) sts at beg of next row,
work 1 row. Cast off 11(12,13) sts at
beg of next and foll alt row. Thread
centre 20 sts onto st holder and work
rem 39(42,45) sts to complete other
side, reversing shapings.

SLEEVES
Rib With 4½mm needles and B, cast
on 37 sts.
Row 1: P2A, k2A, p2A; * to * as back,
twice; k2B, p2A, k2B. Work as for
back.
Inc row P6; (inc in next st, p1) 12
times; p to end [48 sts]. Change to
5mm needles and foll chart as shown
for sleeves at the same time inc 1 st
each end of 4th and every foll 3rd
row until sleeve measures
43(45,47)cm [17(17¾,18½)in] from
beg. Cast off loosely.

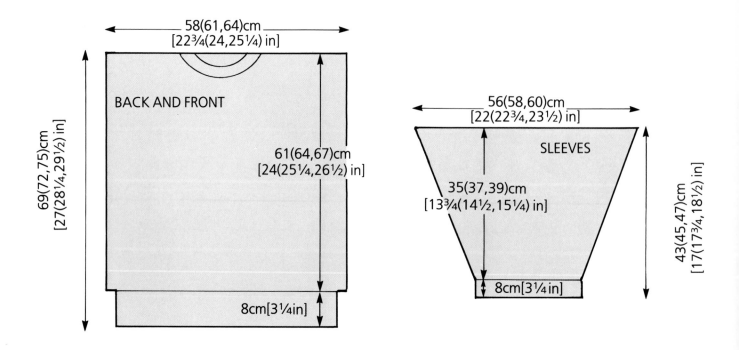

58(61,64)cm
[22¾(24,25¼) in]

BACK AND FRONT

69(72,75)cm
[27(28¼,29½) in]

61(64,67)cm
[24(25¼,26½) in]

8cm[3¼in]

56(58,60)cm
[22(22¾,23½) in]

SLEEVES

35(37,39)cm
[13¾(14½,15¼) in]

43(45,47)cm
[17(17¾,18½) in]

8cm[3¼in]

AEROBICS

SLEEVES

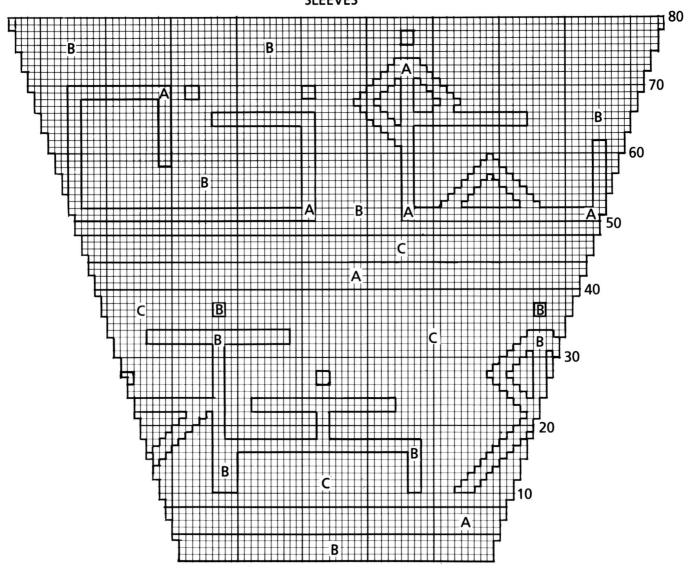

CREW NECK

Join left shoulder using backstitch so that no cast-off sts are visible. With ws facing, using 4½mm needles and A, pup 14 sts down side, 20 sts from front, 14 sts up side and 34 sts from back [82 sts]. Work 8cm [3¼in] as folls: k2A, p2A; * to * as back 6 times; k2B, p2A, k2A. Cast off with B, ribwise, loosely. Join right shoulder and neckband seam, fold collar in half inwards and sew down loosely.

FINISHING OFF

Sew in sleeves by matching centre of each sleeve top with shoulder seam. Sew side and sleeve seams. Press seams if necessary with hot iron and damp cloth, but do not press ribs.

BACK AND FRONT

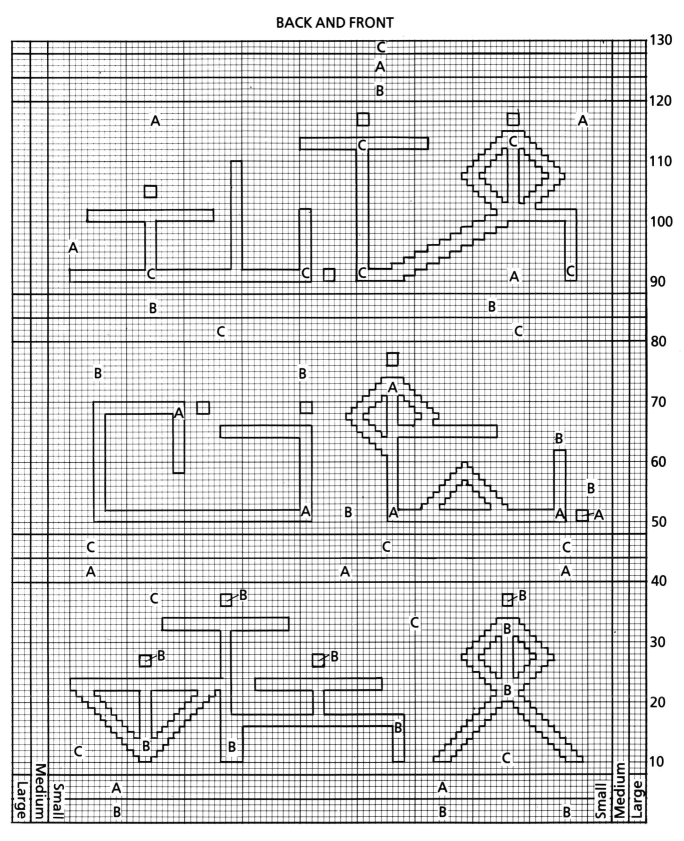

Use small balls or manageable lengths for 'figures'
taking background colour across at back loosely.

ROSE JACKET

*Easy

SIZE
One size only to fit bust 87-98cm [34-38in]

MATERIALS
Yarn used in sample
Kilcarra Classic and Aran
Quantities
Main colour (purple 4030) 15 x 50g balls (A)
contrast (cream [Aran]) 5 x 50g balls (B)
Alternative yarn
Any other Sport or Aran yarn that knits up to same tension
Needles
1 pair each 4½mm (7) and 5mm (6) needles
Buttons
4 x 37mm [1½in] domes

TENSION
Using 5mm (6) needles over stocking stitch, 17/18 sts x 25/26 rows = 10 x 10cm [4 x 4in] (see Tension, page 11).

BACK
Rib With 4½mm needles and B, cast on 110 sts. Work rib as folls:
Row 1: P2A, k2A, p2A; *k2B (using manageable length of yrn or small ball), p2A, k2A, p2A, k2A, p2A*, rep from * to * 8 times altogether; k2B, p2A, k2A, p2A.
Row 2: Starting k2A, p2A, work to match row 1, p B sts. Work 8cm [3¼in], ending with rs row.
Last row: P with A across whole row, but inc 1 st each end of row [112 sts]. Change to 5mm needles.
Now foll charts as given in the foll sequence:
Rows 1-30: Foll 30 rows of chart 1.
Rows 31-40: Plain st st with A.
Rows 41-64: 11A, 20 sts chart 2, 34A, 20 sts chart 2, 26A.
Rows 65-74: Plain st st with A.
Rows 75-98: 26A, 20 sts chart 2, 35A, 20 sts chart 2, 11A.
Rep from row 31 until work measures 65cm [25½in] from beg. K2 rows B (g st). Cast off with B.

FRONTS
Pocket linings (2) With 5mm needles and A, cast on 24 sts and work 34 rows st st. Leave sts on st holder/spare yrn.

Left front
Rib With 4½mm needles and B, cast on 42 sts.
Row 1: P2A; * to * as back, 3 times, k2B, p2A. Work as for back, inc extra 6 sts evenly over last row [48 sts]. Change to 5mm needles and foll 30 rows of chart, noting end sts for left front. Work 4 rows st st with A.
Pocket placing With rs facing, k12, sl next 24 sts onto st holder, k24 sts from pocket lining, k12. Next row: P across all sts, leaving st holder at front of work.
Work 4 more rows plain st st with A, ie ending on row 40.
Cont with patt as folls:
Rows 41-64: 11A, 20 sts chart 2, 17A.
Rows 65-74: St st with A.
Rows 75-98: 17A, 20 sts chart 2, 11A.
Work until front measures 34cm [13½in] from beg, ending with ws row.
Neck shaping Dec 1 st at end of next row and every foll 8th row to 39 sts. Work straight to match length of back, working 2 rows g st with B before casting off.

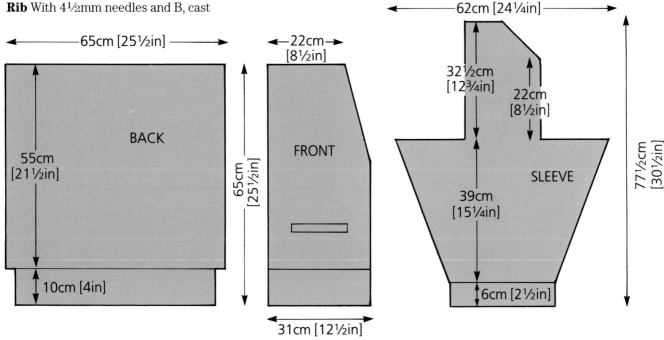

CHART NO 1

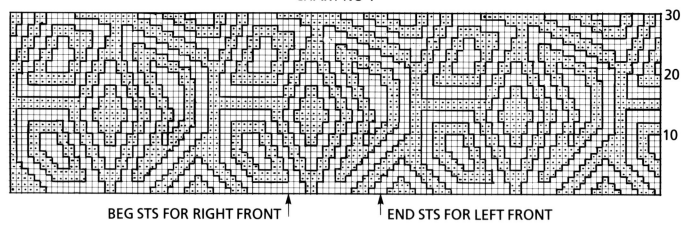

30

20

10

↑
BEG STS FOR RIGHT FRONT | | END STS FOR LEFT FRONT

CHART NO 2

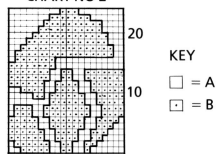

20

10

KEY

☐ = A

⊡ = B

Sew saddle shoulders in place thus

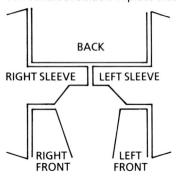

BACK

RIGHT SLEEVE | LEFT SLEEVE

RIGHT FRONT | LEFT FRONT

Right front

As for left, noting beg sts on chart 1 for right front and reversing shapings.

SLEEVES WITH SADDLE SHOULDERS

Rib With 4½mm needles and B, cast on 36 sts.

Row 1: P2A, k2A, p2A; * to * as back, twice, k2B, p2A, k2B. Work as for back.

Inc row P6; (inc in next st, rib 1) 12 times; p to end [48 sts].

Change to 5mm needles and foll charts as foll:

Foundation row 14A, 20 sts chart 2, 14A. Keeping patt correct, inc 1 st each end of 4th and every foll 3rd row until sleeve measures 44cm [17¼in] from beg. Work chart sequence as for back, bringing in new charts as number of sts allow.

Saddle shoulder K to centre 34 sts with B, k34A, rem with B. Next row: K to centre 34 sts with B, k34A, rem with B. Cast off B sts at beg of next 2 rows and work rem 34 sts, keeping patt correct, for a further 23cm [9in].

Left sleeve Rs facing, cast off 1 st at end of next row and 1 st this edge every row to 17 sts. Work straight until saddle shoulder measures 33cm [13in] from cast off edge of sleeve. Cast off with A.

Right sleeve As for left, but reverse saddle-shoulder shaping.

COLLAR AND BUTTON BANDS

Right front

Buttonhole band With rs of right front facing, using 4½mm needles and A, puk 160 sts along edge and work 5 rows k2, p2 rib in A.

Buttonholes (rs facing) Rib 3; (cast off 3, rib 25) 3 times; cast off 3, rib to end. Next row: Rib, casting on 3 sts over those cast off in previous row. Rib further 3 rows.

Collar shaping Change to 5mm needles. **Rib 4, turn, sl 1, rib to end of row. Rib 8, turn, sl 1, rib to end of row. Rib 12, turn, sl 1, rib to end of

row. Cont in this way, working 4 more sts each time, until the row 'rib 64, turn, sl 1, rib to end of row' has been worked**. Cast off all sts with B loosely, ribwise.

Left front

Buttonband As for right, omitting buttonholes and working 11 rows rib. Work rever as right band from ** to ** Cast off with B.

Collar back Join ends of saddle shoulder on left and right sleeve at centre back (see diagram). Set in saddle shoulders of sleeves to cast-off edges of back and fronts. With rs facing, using 4½mm needles and A, puk 50 sts across back of neck. Next row: Working in k2, p2 rib, inc 1 st every other st to 76 sts (inc extra st at end). Cont with rib for 11 rows. Change to 5mm needles and work to match rever length. Cast off with B, loosely, ribwise. Join collar seams.

POCKET TOPS

With 4½mm needles and A, puk 24 sts from st holder and work 6cm [2½in] k2, p2 rib. Cast off with B, ribwise.

FINISHING OFF

Sew pocket linings down inside and neatly secure pocket tops to outside. Sew side and sleeve seams. Sew on buttons to correspond with buttonholes. Press seams if necessary with hot iron and damp cloth, but do not press ribs.

FLOWER BASKET

***Difficult

SIZE
To fit bust 87-92(92-98,98-104)cm
[34-36(36-38,38-40)in]

MATERIALS
Yarn used in sample
Rowan Lightweight DK
Quantities
Main colour (dk grey 61) 17 x 25g
hanks (A)
Basket: (taupe 616) 1 x 25g hank (B)
    (brown 98) 1 x 25g hank (C)
Leaves: (dk green 91) 2 x 25g hanks (D)
    (Turquoise 100)
    1 x 25g hank (E)
Flowers: (purple 94) 2 x 25g hanks (F)
    (lilac 93) 1 x 25g hank (G)
    (yellow 12) 2 x 25g hanks (H)
    (mid brown 604) 1 x 25g
    hank (I)
    (dk brown 117) 1 x 25g
    hank (J)
    (red 45) 1 x 25g hank (K)
    (rust 26) 1 x 25g hank (L)
    (lt blue 55) 2 x 25g hanks (M)
    (lemon 116) 1 x 25g hank (N)

Alternative yarn
Any DK that knits up to same tension
Needles
1 pair each 3¼mm (10) and 4mm
(8) needles
1 cable needle for ribs
1 circular needle 3¼mm (10) for
collar

TENSION
Using 4mm (8) needles over stocking
stitch, 24 sts x 32 rows =
10 x 10cm [4 x 4in] (see Tension,
page 11).

BACK
Rib With 3¼mm needles and A, cast
on 99(107,115) sts and work rib as
folls:
Row 1: *P1; (k1, p1) 4(6,8) times*;
[k1, p1, c2b, k1, c2f, p1, k1; (p1, k1) 7
times; p1] 4 times, but ending (p1,
k1) 4(6,8) times, p1 on last rep.
Row 2: *K1; (p1, k1) 4(6,8) times*;
[p1, k1, p5, k1, p1; (k1, p1) 7 times;
k1] 4 times, ending (k1, p1) 4(6,8)
times, k1 on last rep.
Row 3: As row 1 * to *; [k1, c2b, k3,
c2f, k1; (p1, k1) 7 times; p1] 4 times,
ending as row 1.
Row 4: As row 2 * to *; [p9; (k1, p1) 7
times; k1] 4 times, ending as row 2.
Row 5: As row 1 * to *; [c2b, k5, c2f;
(p1, k1) 7 times; p1] 4 times etc.
Row 6: As row 4.
Row 7: As row 1 * to *; [k9; (p1, k1) 7
times; p1] 4 times etc.
Row 8: As row 4.
Row 9: As row 1 * to *; [c2f, k5, c2b;
(p1, k1) 7 times; p1] 4 times etc.
Row 10: As row 4.
Row 11: As row 1 * to *; [k1, c2f, k3,
c2b, k1; (p1, k1) 7 times; p1] 4 times
etc.
Row 12: As row 2.
Row 13: As row 1 * to *; [k1, p1, c2f,
k1, c2b, p1, k1; (p1, k1) 7 times; p1] 4
times etc.
Row 14: As row 2.
Row 15: As row 1 * to *; [k1, p1, k1,
c3f, k1, p1, k1; (p1, k1) 7 times; p1] 4
times etc.
Row 16: As row 2.

These 16 rows form rib patt. Rep
them once more, inc extra sts on last
row thus:
Inc row Rib 5(11,17), (inc in next st,
rib 2) 29 times, rib to end
[128(136,144) sts]. Change to 4mm

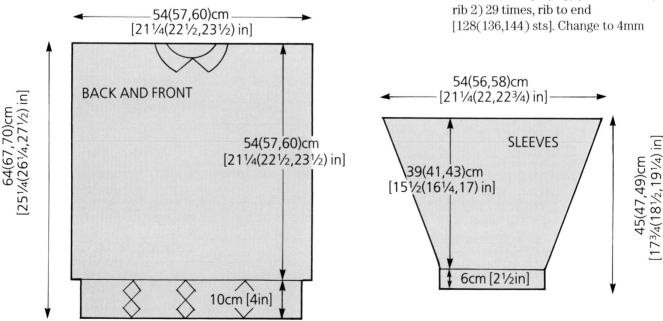

54(57,60)cm
[21¼(22½,23½) in]

BACK AND FRONT

64(67,70)cm
[25¼(26¼,27½) in]

54(57,60)cm
[21¼(22½,23½) in]

10cm [4in]

54(56,58)cm
[21¼(22,22¾) in]

SLEEVES

39(41,43)cm
[15½(16¼,17) in]

45(47,49)cm
[17¾(18½,19¼) in]

6cm [2½in]

FRONT

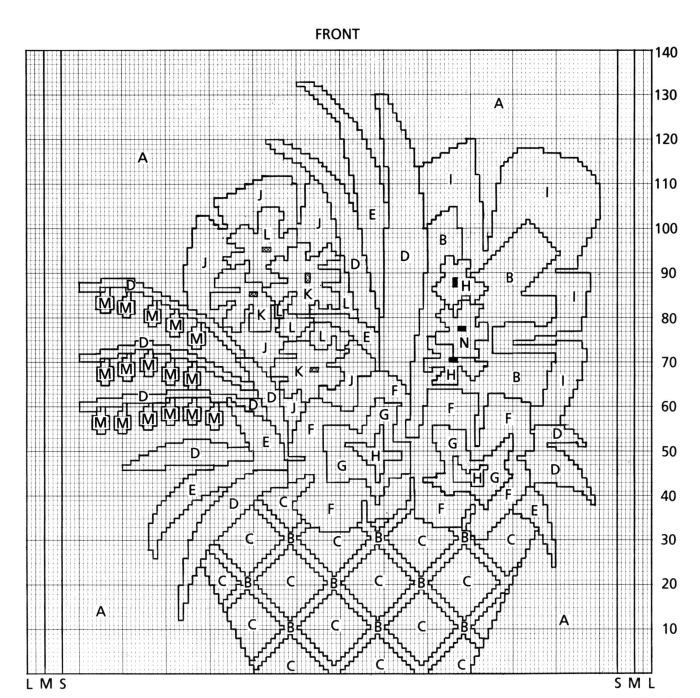

L M S   S M L

needles and foll chart as given for back thus: work first 16 rows of border followed by 84 rows of flower patt. These 84 rows are then repeated until the correct measurement has been reached. Work to 62(65,68)cm [24¼(25½,26¾)in] from beg. **Shoulder shaping** Cast off 10(11,12) sts at beg of next 4 rows,

and 11(12,13) sts at beg of foll 4 rows. Leave rem 44 sts on st holder/ spare yrn.

FRONT
As for back but foll chart given for front thus: work the 16 rows of border as shown on chart for back; work 2(6,10) rows plain st st in A then foll chart until the correct

KEY FOR FRONT:- ⊠ = J ■ = C

measurement has been reached. Work until front measures 55(58,61)cm [21½(22¾,24)in] from beg.
Neck shaping Patt first 51(55,59) sts, turn. Dec 1 st at neck edge next and every alt row to 42(46,50) sts, ending with a p row. Work to

BACK AND SLEEVES

SLEEVES SLEEVES

A A A

D D D

A A A

D D D

A A

100
90
80
70
60
50
40
30
20
10

L M S   KEY FOR BORDER PATTERN:- □ = F ⊡ =H   S M L

PETALS (BACK AND SLEEVES):-
At □ = with M, K1, P1, K1, all in next st, turn, inc 1 st, P to end, inc 1 st, turn, work 3 rows st st, turn, dec 1 st each end of next row turn, slip 1, K2tog, PSSO. Leave st on needle and knit in at ⊠ .

62(65,68)cm [24¼(25½,26¾)in] from beg.
Shoulder shaping Cast off 10(11,12) sts at beg of next and foll alt row, work 1 row. Cast off 11(12,13) sts at beg of next and foll alt row. Sl centre 26 sts onto safety pin and work rem sts to match left side, reversing shapings.

SLEEVES
Rib With 3¼mm needles and A, cast on 49 sts and work rib as for back starting thus:
Row 1: (K1, p1) 4 times; [k1, p1, c2b, k1, c2f, p1, k1; (p1, k1) 7 times; p1] twice, ending (p1, k1) 4 times. Now work as given for back on sts as set. Work 15 rows.
Inc row Work as row 16 but inc extra sts as folls: rib 1; (rib 1, inc in next st) 23 times, rib to end [72 sts]. Change to 4mm needles and foll chart for sleeve (as back), at the same time inc 1 st each end of 5th and every foll 4th row to end until sleeves measure 45(47,49)cm [17(17¾,18½)in] from beg. Cast off loosely.

COLLAR
Join both shoulders using backstitch so that no cast-off sts are visible. With 3¼mm circular needle, starting in centre of front, puk 13 sts from front, 25 sts up side, 44 sts from back, 25 sts down side and 13 sts from front [120 sts]. Mark end of row with contrast yrn. Work 6 rows k1, p1 rib in rounds, ending above marked st. Now work in rows, thus dividing for collar. Cont in k1, p1 rib for a further 8cm [3¼in]. Cast off neatly, ribwise.

FINISHING OFF
Press all pieces using hot iron and damp cloth before joining together. Sew in sleeves matching centre of each sleeve top with shoulder seam. Press these seams. Sew side and sleeve seams, using backstitch or invisible grafting st. Press rem seams, but do not press ribs.

BEAUTY SPOT

**Needs some experience

SIZE
To fit bust 87-92(92-98,98-104)cm [34-36(36-38,38-40)in]

MATERIALS
Yarn used in sample
Jaeger Sport
Quantities
Main colour (cream 220) 12 x 50g (A)
1st contrast (wild rose 250) 2 x 50g (B)
2nd contrast (black 216) 2 x 50g (C)
3rd contrast (mole 235) 7 x 50g (D)
Alternative yarn
Any Sport or Aran type yarn that knits up to same tension
Needles
1 pair each 4½mm (7) and 5mm (6) needles
1 4½mm (7) circular needle

TENSION
Using 5mm (6) needles over stocking stitch, 17/18 sts x 26 rows = 10 x 10cm [4 x 4in] (see Tension, page 11).

Tip The back and front are mirror images of each other. Knit back first then, whilst working front reading the chart in opposite direction, lay the back down, wrong side up, so that you can see more clearly what front should look like as you knit it.

BACK
Rib With 4½mm needles and B, cast on 68(74,80) sts and work k2, p2 rib as folls:
Row 1: 1st & 3rd size only: k2A, p2A; all sizes: *k2B (using manageable lengths or small balls), p2A, k2A, p2A, k2A, p2A*, rep from * to * 5(6,6) times; k2B, p2A (k2B; k2B, p2A).
Row 2: Work to match row 1, p B sts. Work 8cm [3¼in] ending with rs row.
Inc row P4(7,10); (p1, inc in next st) 30 times; p to end [98(104,110) sts]. Change to 5mm needles. Now foll chart as given for back, noting beg and end sts for each size. Work until back measures 67(70,73)cm [26¼(27½,28¾)in] from beg.
Shoulder shaping Cast off

10(11,12) sts at beg of next 2 rows. Cast off 11(12,13) sts at beg of foll 4 rows. Leave rem 34 sts on st holder/ spare yrn.

FRONT
As for back reversing chart, and working until it measures 60(63,66)cm [23½(24¾,26)in] from beg.
Neck shaping Patt first 39(42,45) sts, turn and dec 1 st at beg of next and every foll alt row to 32(35,38) sts. Cont straight until front measures same as back.
Shoulder shaping Cast off 10(11,12) sts at beg of next row, work 1 row. Cast off 11(12,13) sts at beg of next and foll alt row. Thread centre 20 sts onto st holder and work rem 39(42,45) sts to complete other side, reversing shapings.

SLEEVES
Rib With 4½mm needles and B, cast on 36 sts.
Row 1: P2A, k2A, p2A; * to * as back,

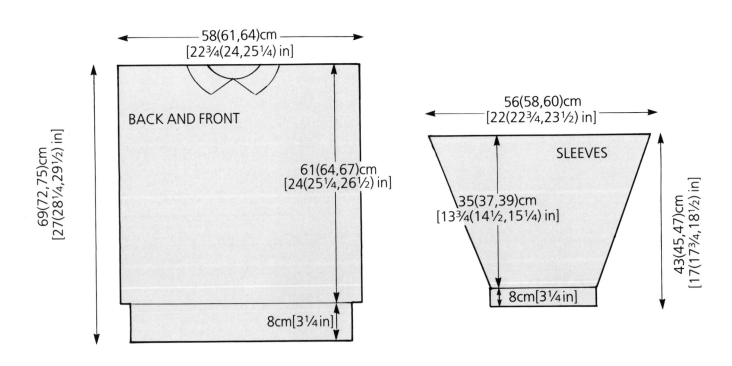

58(61,64)cm
[22¾(24,25¼) in]

BACK AND FRONT

69(72,75)cm
[27(28¼,29½) in]

61(64,67)cm
[24(25¼,26½) in]

8cm[3¼in]

56(58,60)cm
[22(22¾,23½) in]

SLEEVES

35(37,39)cm
[13¾(14½,15¼) in]

43(45,47)cm
[17(17¾,18½) in]

8cm[3¼in]

BACK AND FRONT

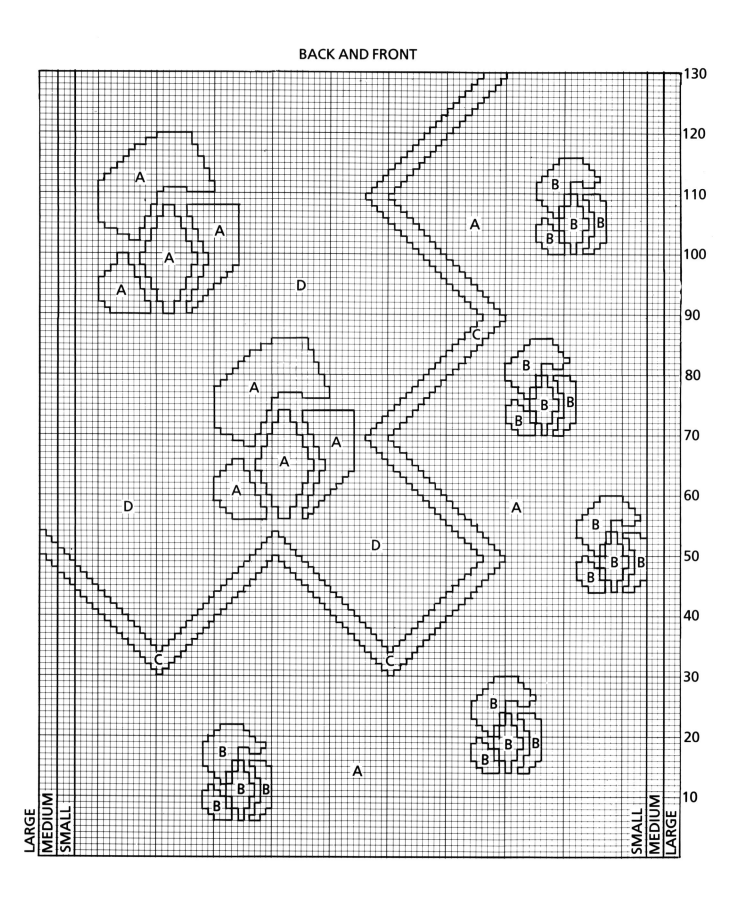

RIGHT SLEEVE

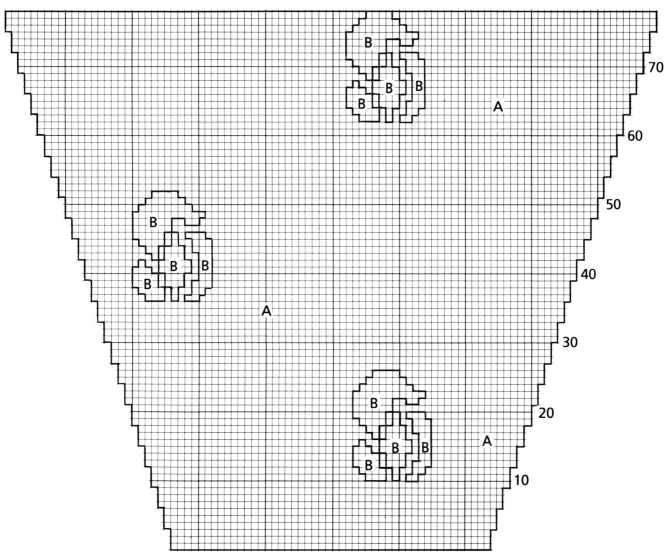

BACK K rows work from right to left;
   P rows work from left to right
FRONT (Mirror image)
   K rows work from left to right
   P rows work from right to left

LEFT SLEEVE

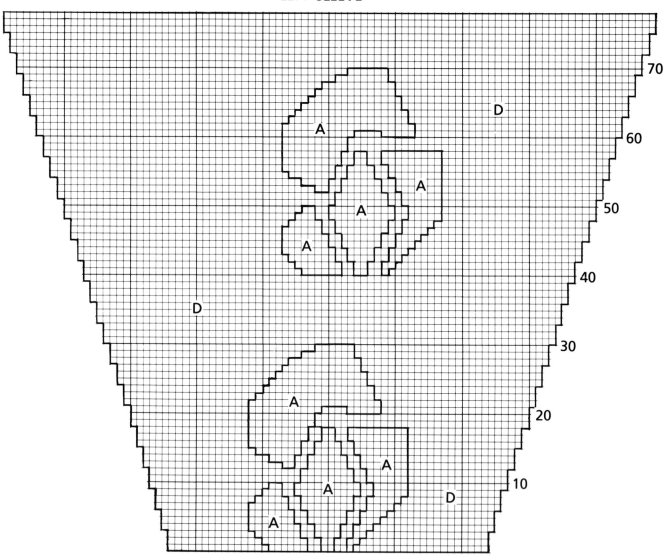

twice, k2B, p2A, k2B. Work as for back.
Inc row P6, (inc in next st, p1) 12 times; p to end [48 sts]. Change to 5mm needles and foll charts as given for each sleeve, at the same time inc 1 st each end of 4th and every foll 3rd row until sleeve measures 43(45,47)cm [17(17¾,18½)in] from beg. Cast off loosely.

LITTLE COLLAR
Join both shoulders using backstitch so that no cast-off sts are visible. With ws facing, using 4½mm circular needle and A, starting in centre of front, pup 10 sts from front, 14 sts up side, 34 sts from back, 14 sts down side and 10 sts from front (82 sts). Mark end of row with contrast yarn. Keeping ws facing, work rib in rounds as folls: p1A, k2A, p2A: * to * as back, 6 times; k2B, p2A, k2A, p1A. Work

this row 4 times, ending above the marked st. Now work in rows, thus dividing for collar. Cont in rib for a further 8cm [3¼in]. Cast off with B, loosely, ribwise.

FINISHING OFF
Sew in sleeves, matching centre of each sleeve top with shoulder seam, sew side and sleeve seams. Press seams if necessary with hot iron and damp cloth, but do not press ribs.

DOUBLE KNITTING CABLE

*Easy

SIZE
To fit bust 87-92(92-98,98-104)cm
[34-36(36-38,38-40)in]

MATERIALS
Yarn used in sample
Anne Rowena DK
Quantity
18 x 50g balls
Alternative yarn
Any DK that knits up to same tension
Needles
1 pair each 3¼mm (10) and 4mm
(8) needles
1 cable needle
Buttons
4 x 14mm [½in] domes

TENSION
Using 4mm (8) needles over cable
pattern, 35 sts x 32 rows = 10 x 10cm
[4 x 4in] (see Tension, page 11).

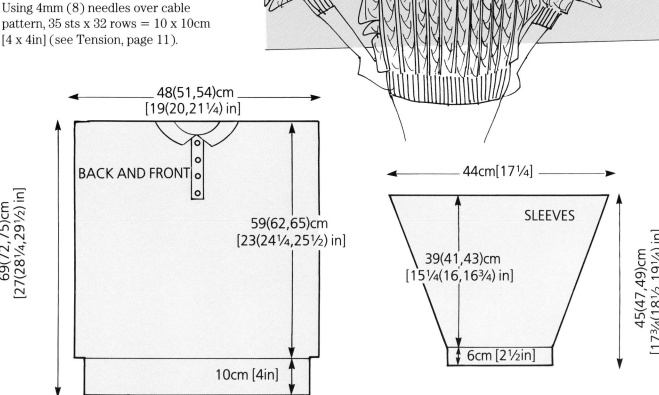

48(51,54)cm
[19(20,21¼) in]

BACK AND FRONT

69(72,75)cm
[27(28¼,29½) in]

59(62,65)cm
[23(24¼,25½) in]

10cm [4in]

44cm[17¼]

SLEEVES

39(41,43)cm
[15¼(16,16¾) in]

45(47,49)cm
[17¾(18½,19¼) in]

6cm [2½in]

BACK

Rib With 3¼mm needles cast on 98(106,114) sts and work 10cm [4in] k1, p1 rib.

Inc row Rib 4(8,12) sts; (inc in next st, rib 2) 30 times; rib to end [128(136,144) sts]. Change to 4mm needles. Foll patt thus:

Row 1: (Foundation row; omit inc sts on all reps of this row). P1(2,0); *k1, (inc in next st) twice, k1, p2* rep from * to * 21(22,24) times; k1(2,0) [170(180,192) sts].

Row 2 and every alt row: K1(2,0); *k2, p6* rep from * to * 21(22,24) times; k1(2,0).

Row 3: P1(2,0); *k6, p2* rep from * to * 21(22,24) times; k1(2,0).

Row 5: P1(2,0); *c6b (sl next 3 sts onto cable needle and hold at back of work, k3, k 3 sts from cable needle), p2* 21(22,24) times; k1(2,0).

Row 7: As row 3.

Row 8: As row 2.

These 8 rows form patt and are repeated throughout**. Work until back measures 67(70,73)cm [26¼(27½,28¾)in] from beg.

Shoulder shaping Important: to keep shape of jumper correct, you must dec the sts inc on foundation row when you shape for shoulders (ie * to * will be *k1, k2tog twice, k1, p2*, taking the number of sts back to 6 again). The number of sts given for casting off are those *after* dec allowed for (ie k2tog counted as 1 st). Cast off 10(11,12) sts at beg of next 4 rows, and 11(12,13) sts at beg of foll 4 rows. Work rem sts once more dec foundation sts leaving 44 sts in total. Leave these sts on st holder/spare yrn.

FRONT

As for back to **. Work to 42(45,48)cm [16½(17¾,19)in] from beg. Patt first 80(85,91) sts. Turn, patt further 18 sts on these sts only, ending with rs row.

Neck shaping Work next 10 sts then transfer these to safety pin. Dec 1 st at neck edge every alt row to 56(60,66) sts, dec foundation sts at same time. Work to measure same length as back to shoulder shaping, ending with ws row.

Shoulder shaping (Work as for back). Cast off 10(11,12) sts at beg of next and foll alt row, work 1 row. Cast off 11(12,13) sts at beg of next and foll alt row. Sl centre 10 sts onto pin and work rem sts to match left side, reversing shapings.

SLEEVES

Rib With 3¼mm needles, cast on 48 sts and work k1, p1 rib for 6cm [2½in].

Inc row (Rib 1, inc in next st) to end [72 sts]. Foll patt as for back starting *p2, k1 (inc in next st) twice, k1*, rep from * to * 12 times, at the same time inc 1 st each end of 5th and every foll 4th row to end – inc additional sts for cable patt as you come to them. When sleeve measures 45(47,49)cm [17¾(18¼,19¼)in] from beg, cast off loosely, pattwise, k2tog over inc sts on foundation row.

BUTTON BAND

(Left side): sl centre 10 sts of front onto 3¼mm needle. Work k1, p1 rib until band measures up to beg of neck shaping when slightly stretched. With ws facing, cast off first 5 sts and leave rem 5 sts on pin. Graft band in place. Mark 4 button placings evenly along band, top and bottom ones 1cm [⅜in] from top and bottom edges.

BUTTONHOLE BAND

(Right side): puk 10 sts from front again and work as for button band but work buttonholes to correspond with button placings.

Buttonhole Rs facing, rib 4, yrn fwd, k2tog, rib to end. Rib next row. End with rs facing, cast off 5 sts, leave 5 sts on safety pin.

COLLAR

Join both shoulders using backstitch so that no cast-off sts are visible. With rs facing, starting with buttonhole band, puk 5 sts, then 8 sts from front (k2tog twice over cable patt), 28 sts up side, 44 sts from back, 28 sts down side, 8 sts from left front (k2tog twice over cable patt) and 5 from buttonband [126 sts]. Work 8cm [3¼in] k1, p1 rib. Cast off loosely, ribwise.

FINISHING OFF

Sew in sleeves, matching each sleeve top with shoulder seam. Sew side and sleeve seams, press seams gently with hot iron and damp cloth, taking care not to press cables or ribs. Sew buttons in place.

GARDEN PARTY

***Difficult

SIZE
To fit bust 87-92(92-98,98-104)cm [34-36(36-38,38-40)in]

MATERIALS
Yarn used in sample
Jaeger Matchmaker 2 DK
Quantities
Main colour (lt natural 663) 11 x 50g balls (A)
1st contrast (china pink 677) 3 x 50g balls (B)
2nd contrast (gun metal 726) 2 x 50g balls (C)
3rd contrast (aster 721) 2 x 50g balls (D)
4th contrast (water crest 670) 2 x 50g balls (E)
Alternative yarn
Any DK yarn that knits up to same tension
Needles
1 pair each 3¼mm (10) and 4mm (8) needles

TENSION
Using 4mm (8) needles over stocking stitch, 24 sts x 32 rows = 10 x 10cm [4 x 4in] (see Tension, page 11).

BACK
Rib With 3¼mm needles and A, cast on 110(118,126) sts and work cable rib as folls:
Rows 1,3 & 5: P2(3,3); *p1, k6, p1, c6b&f – (ie sl 2 sts onto cable needle and hold at back of work, k1, k sts off cable needle, sl 1 onto cable needle and hold at front of work, k2, k st from cable needle)*. Rep from * to * 7(8,8) times, p1(3,1); k6(0,6); p3(0,4).
Row 2 and every alt row: K p sts and p k sts.
Rows 7,9 & 11: P2(3,3); * p1, c6b&f, p1, k6* reap from * to * 7(8,8) times; p1(3,1); 1st and 3rd sizes only c6b&f, p3(0,4).
Row 12: As row 2.
These 12 rows form rib patt repeat.
When rib measures 10cm [4in] from beg, with ws row facing, inc 18 sts evenly over last row to 128(136,144) sts. Change to 4mm needles and foll chart as given noting beg and end sts for each size. Work until back measures 62(65,68)cm

[24¼(25½,26¾in] from beg.
Shoulder shaping Cast off 10(11,12) sts at beg of next 4 rows and 11(12,13) sts at beg of foll 4 rows. Leave rem 44 sts on st holder/ spare yrn.

FRONT
As for back but work to 55(58,61)cm [21½(23,24)in] from beg.
Neck shaping Patt first 51(55,59) sts, turn. Dec 1 st at neck edge next and every alt row to 42(46,50) sts, ending with p row. Work straight to match back length.
Shoulder shaping Cast off 10(11,12) sts at beg of next and foll alt row, work 1 row. Cast off 11(12,13) sts at beg of next and foll alt row. Leave centre 26 sts on st holder and work rem sts to match left side, reversing all shapings.

SLEEVES
Rib With 3¼mm needles and A, cast on 58 sts and work cable rib as folls:
Foundation row: (rs) P1 *p1, k6, p1, c6b&f*. Rep from * to * 4 times, p1. Work rib as for back on sts as set. Work 11 rows only.
Inc row Working in patt, inc 14 sts evenly over last row, ie (work 3, inc in next st) 14 times, work to end of row [72 sts].

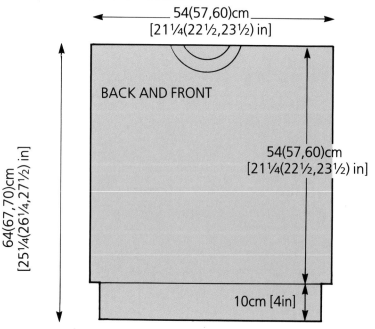

54(57,60)cm
[21¼(22½,23½) in]

BACK AND FRONT

54(57,60)cm
[21¼(22½,23½) in]

64(67,70)cm
[25¼(26¼,27½) in]

10cm [4in]

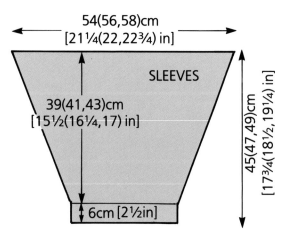

54(56,58)cm
[21¼(22,22¾) in]

SLEEVES

39(41,43)cm
[15½(16¼,17) in]

45(47,49)cm
[17¾(18½,19¼) in]

6cm [2½in]

SLEEVES

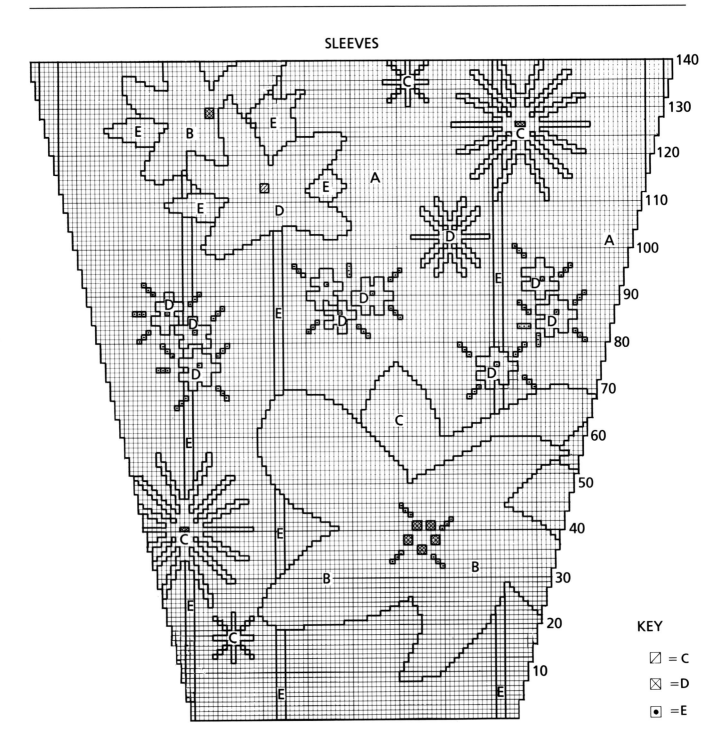

KEY

◨ = C

⊠ = D

⊡ = E

Change to 4mm needles and foll chart as given for sleeves, at the same time inc 1 st each end of 5th and every foll 4th row until sleeve measures 45(47,49)cm [17¾(18½,19¼)in] from beg. Cast off loosely.

CREW NECK
Join left shoulder using backstitch so that no cast-off sts are visible. With rs facing, using 3¼mm needles and A, puk 44 sts from back, 28 sts down left side, 26 sts from front and 28 sts up right side [126 sts]. Work 6cm [2½in] k1, p1 rib, cast off loosely, ribwise. Join right shoulder and neckband seam. Fold collar in half inwards and sew down – secure but not too tight.

FINISHING OFF
Press each piece separately before sewing up, using hot iron and damp cloth. Set in sleeves matching centre of each sleeve top to shoulder seam. Sew side and sleeve seams, press seams. If cable rib curls up slightly, press very gently with damp cloth.

FLOWERING DELIGHT

***Difficult

SIZE
To fit bust 87-92(92-98,98-104)cm [34-36(36-38,38-40)in]

MATERIALS
Yarn used in sample
Rowan Lightweight DK
Quantities
Main colour (taupe 616) 15 x 25g hanks (A)
1st contrast (dk brown 117) 4 x 25g hanks (B)
2nd contrast (ecru 84) 3 x 25g hanks (C)
3rd contrast (red 45) 2 x 25g hanks (D)
4th contrast (brown 98) 1 x 25g hank (E)
5th contrast (mid brown 604) 2 x 25g hanks (F)
6th contrast (rust 26) 1 x 25g hank (G)
Alternative yarn
Any DK that knits up to same tension
Needles
1 pair each 3¼mm (10) and 4mm (8) needles
1 cable needle for ribs

TENSION
Using 4mm (8) needles over stocking stitch, 24sts x 32 rows = 10 x 10cm [4 x 4in] (see Tension, page 11).

BACK
Rib With 3¼mm needles and A, cast on 99(107,115) sts and work rib as folls:
Row 1: *P1; (k1, p1) 4(6,8) times*; [k1, p1, c2b, k1, c2f, p1, k1; (p1, k1) 7 times; p1] 4 times, but ending (p1, k1) 4 (6,8) times, p1 on last rep.
Row 2: *K1; (p1, k1) 4(6,8) times*; [p1, k1, p5, k1, p1; (k1, p1) 7 times; k1] 4 times, ending (k1, p1) 4(6,8) times, k1 on last rep.
Row 3: As row 1 * to *; [k1, c2b, k3, c2f, k1; (p1, k1) 7 times; p1] 4 times, ending as row 1.
Row 4: As row 2 * to *; [p9; (k1, p1) 7 times; k1] 4 times, ending as row 2.
Row 5: As row 1 * to *; [c2b, k5, c2f; (p1, k1) 7 times; p1] 4 times etc.
Row 6: As row 4.
Row 7: As row 1 * to *; [k9; (p1, k1) 7 times; p1] 4 times etc.
Row 8: As row 4.
Row 9: As row 1 * to *; [c2f, k5, c2b; (p1, k1) 7 times; p1] 4 times etc.
Row 10: As row 4.
Row 11: As row 1 * to *; [k1, c2f, k3, c2b, k1; (p1, k1) 7 times; p1] 4 times etc.
Row 12: As row 2.
Row 13: As row 1 * to *; [k1, p1, c2f, k1, c2b, p1, k1; (p1, k1) 7 times; p1] 4 times etc.
Row 14: As row 2.
Row 15: As row 1 * to *; [k1, p1, k1, c3f, k1, p1, k1; (p1, k1) 7 times; p1] 4 times etc.
Row 16: As row 2.
These 16 rows form rib patt. Rep them once more, inc extra sts on last row thus:
Inc row Rib 5(11,17); (inc in next st, rib 2) 29 times; rib to end [128(136,144) sts]. Change to 4mm needles and foll chart as given for back. Work to 62(65,68)cm [24¼(25½,26¾)in] from beg.
Shoulder shaping Cast off 10(11,12) sts at beg of next 4 rows, and 11(12,13) sts at beg of foll 4 rows. Leave rem 44 sts on st holder/spare yrn.

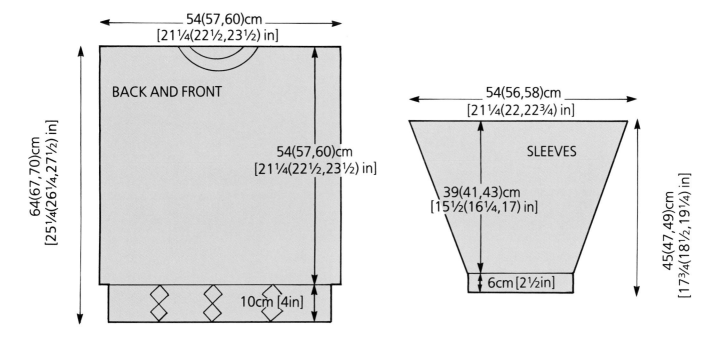

62(65,68)cm [24¼(25½,26¾)in]
from beg.
Shoulder shaping Cast off
10(11,12) sts at beg of next and foll
alt row, work 1 row. Cast off
11(12,13) sts at beg of next and foll
alt row. Sl centre 26 sts onto safety
pin and work rem sts to match left
side, reversing shapings.

SLEEVES
Rib With 3¼mm needles and A, cast
on 49 sts and work rib as for back
starting thus:
Row 1: (K1, p1) 4 times; [k1, p1, c2b,
k1, c2f, p1, k1; (p1, k1) 7 times; p1]
twice, ending (p1, k1) 4 times. Now
work as given for back on sts as set.
Work 15 rows.
Inc row Work as row 16 but inc extra
sts as folls: rib 1; (rib 1, inc in next st)
23 times; rib to end [72 sts]. Change
to 4mm needles and foll chart for
sleeves but at the same time inc 1 st
each end of 5th and every foll 4th row
until sleeve measures 45(47,49)cm
[17¾(18½,19¼)in] from beg. Cast
off loosely.

NECKBAND
Join left shoulder using backstitch so
that no cast-off sts are visible. With rs
facing, using 3¼mm needles and A,
puk 44 sts from back, 25 sts down left
side, 26 sts from front and 25 sts up
right side [120 sts]. Work rib as given
for back starting thus (ws facing):
[P1, k1, p5, k1, p1; (k1, p1) 7 times;
k1] 5 times. Now work from row 3 of
back on sts as set. Work to row 15.
Cast off patternwise, neatly. Join
right shoulder and neckband seam.

FINISHING OFF
Press all pieces using hot iron and
damp cloth before joining together.
Set in sleeves matching centre of
each sleeve top with shoulder seam.
Press these seams. Sew side and
sleeve seams, using backstitch or
invisible grafting st. Press rem seams,
but do not press ribs.

FRONT
As for back until work measures
55(58,61)cm [21½(22¾,24)in] from
beg.
Neck shaping Patt first 51(55,59)
sts, turn. Dec 1 st at neck edge next
and every alt row to 42(46,50) sts,
ending with a p row. Work to

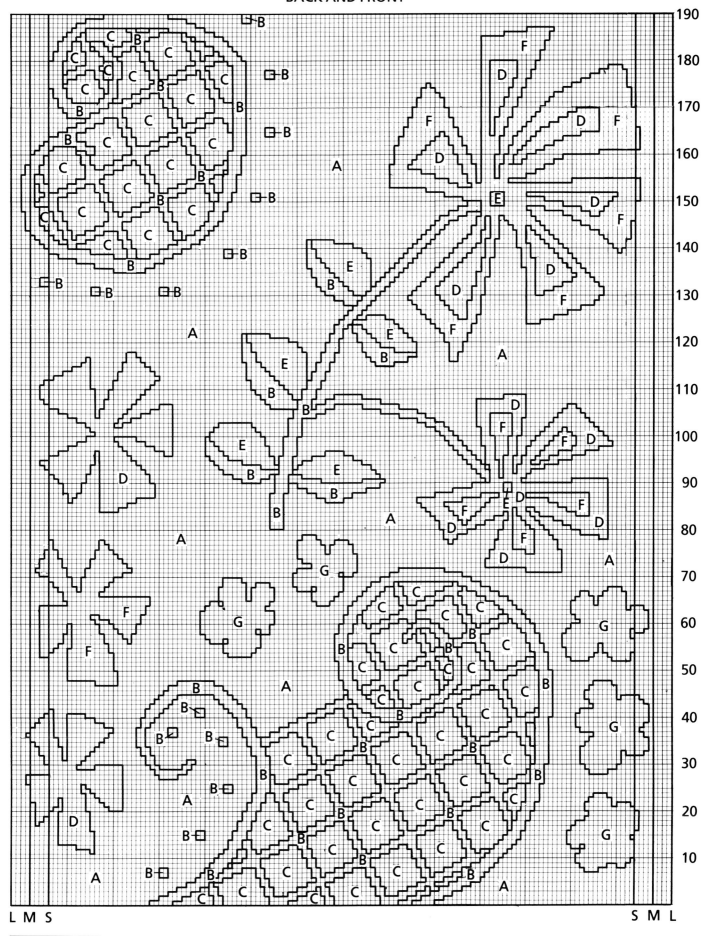

SLEEVES

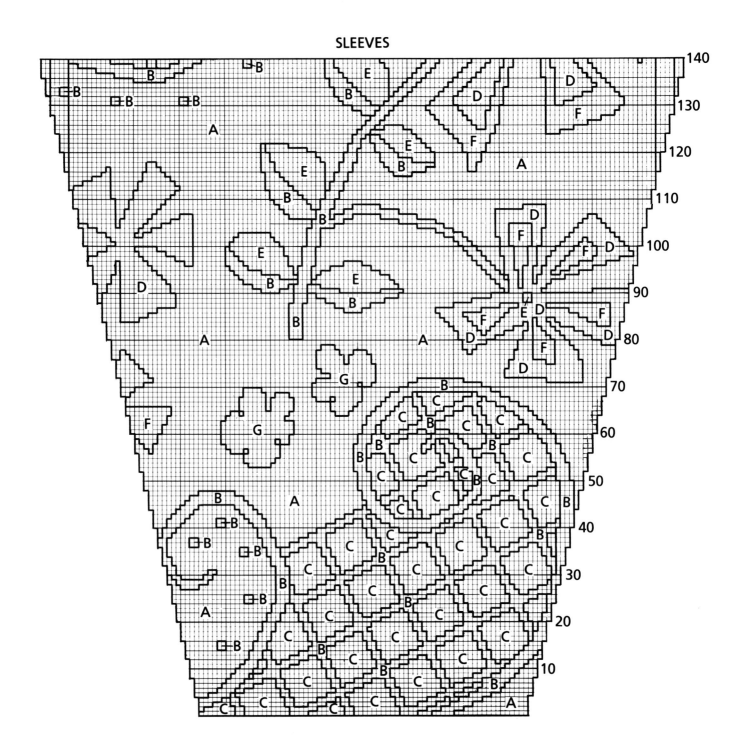

PLAIN 4 PLY

SIZE
To fit bust 87-92(92-98,98-104)cm
[34-36(36-38,38-40)in]

MATERIALS
Yarn used in sample
Jaeger Angora
Quantity
19(20,21) x 25g balls
Alternative yarn
Any 4 ply yarn that knits up to same
tension
Needles
1 pair each 3mm (11) and 3¼mm
(10) needles
Buttons
4 buttons approx 14mm [½in] for
shirt collar, plus 1 for pocket

TENSION
Using 3¼mm (10) needles over
stocking stitch, 30sts x 40 rows =
10 x 10cm [4 x 4in] (see Tension,
page 11).

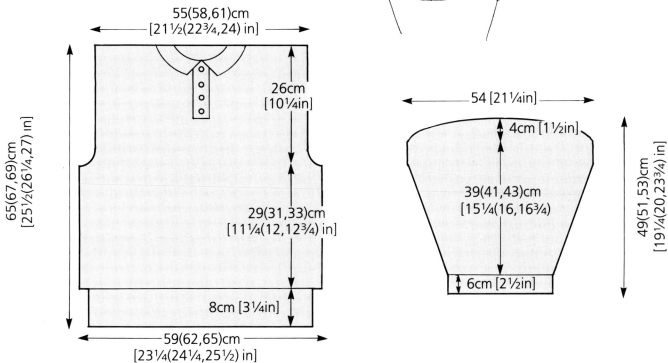

55(58,61)cm
[21½(22¾,24) in]

26cm
[10¼in]

65(67,69)cm
[25½(26¼,27) in]

29(31,33)cm
[11¼(12,12¾) in]

8cm [3¼in]

59(62,65)cm
[23¼(24¼,25½) in]

54 [21¼in]

4cm [1½in]

39(41,43)cm
[15¼(16,16¾)

49(51,53)cm
[19¼(20,23¾) in]

6cm [2½in]

Note This pattern gives a basic plain 4 ply jumper with the choice of three different collars – crew neck, shirt collar or little collar. Use this pattern in conjunction with the charts for Five-Square Jumper and 4 Ply Lines (pp130,134) for variation.

BACK

Rib With 3mm needles, cast on 158(166,174) sts and work 8cm [3¼in] k1, p1 rib, inc 20 sts evenly over last row to 178(186,194) sts. Change to 3¼mm needles and work in plain st st (1 row k, 1 row p) until work measures 37(39,41)cm [14½(15¼,16)in] from beg.
Armhole shaping K2tog at each end of next row and foll alt row. P next row. K2tog each end of next and every 4th row to 166(174,182) sts * Cont straight until armhole measures 26cm [10¼in] from beg of shaping.
Shoulder shaping Cast off 13(14,15) sts at beg of next 6 rows, 14(15,16) sts at beg of foll 2 rows, leaving rem 60 sts on st holder/spare yrn.

FRONT FOR CREW NECK AND LITTLE COLLAR

As for back to *. Cont straight until armhole measures 19cm [7½in] from beg of shaping.
Neck shaping Patt first 67(71,75) sts. Turn. ** Dec 1 st at neck edge on next and every row to 53(57,61) sts. Work to measure same length as back.
Shoulder shaping Cast off 13(14,15) sts at beg of next and foll alt 2 rows, work 1 row, cast off rem 14(15,16) sts **. Leave centre 32 sts on st holder and work rem sts to match left side, reversing shapings.

FRONT FOR SHIRT COLLAR

As for back to *. Work a further 5cm [2in] from beg of armhole shaping. Patt first 80(84,88) sts. Turn and cont on these sts only to 19cm [7½in] from beg of armhole shaping, ending with rs row. Sl first 13 sts onto safety pin and foll shaping as given above in Crew Neck Front from ** to **. Sl centre 6 sts onto safety pin and work rem sts to match left side, reversing shapings.

SLEEVES

Rib With 3mm needles, cast on 62 sts. Work 6cm [2½in] k1, p1 rib, inc 30 sts evenly over last row to 92 sts. Change to 3¼mm needles and work plain st st as for back, at the same time inc 1 st each end of 5th and every foll 4th row to 164 sts. Work straight until sleeve measures 45(47,49)cm [17¾(18½,19¼)in] from beg.
Top shaping Dec 1 st each end of every alt row to 146 sts. Cast off loosely.

CREW NECK

Join left shoulder using backstitch so that no cast-off sts are visible. With rs facing, using 3mm needles, puk 60 sts from back, 18 sts down side, 32 sts from front and 18 sts up side [128 sts] ***. Work 7cm[2¾in] st st, with rs facing outwards. Join right shoulder and neckband using backstitch; fold neckband in half inwards and sew down inside.

LITTLE COLLAR

As for Crew Neck to ***. Work 4 rows k1, p1 rib and cast off loosely, ribwise. With 3mm needles cast on 132 sts. Work 8cm [3¼in] k1, p1 rib, cast off loosely, ribwise. Join right shoulder and neckband. Sew collar inside neckband, at base of ribbing, ensuring that collar opening lies at centre front.

SHIRT COLLAR

Buttonband With 3mm needles, puk centre 6 sts from safety pin. With rs facing, work k1, p1 rib inc 1 st at end of first row to 7 sts. Work band to measure to beg of neck shaping when slightly stretched. Leave sts on safety pin and graft band in place. Sew 4 buttons evenly spaced along band.
Buttonhole band Puk centre 6 sts again, in front of buttonband. Work as for buttonband but make buttonholes to correspond with button placings.
Buttonhole (rs facing) Rib 3, yrn fwd, k2tog, rib 2. Graft band in place, leaving sts on pin.
Collar Join both shoulders using backstitch so that no cast-off sts are visible. Starting with buttonhole band, with rs facing, using 3mm needles, puk 7 sts from band, 13 sts from right front, 32 sts up side, 60 sts from back, 32 sts down side, 13 sts from left front and 7 sts from band [164 sts]. Work 8cm [3¼in] k1, p1 rib. Cast off loosely, ribwise.

POCKET

With 3¼mm needles cast on 30 sts and work 40 rows st st. Change to 3mm needles and work 2 rows k1, p1 rib.
Buttonhole row Rib 14, yrn fwd, k2tog, rib to end. Rib 1 more row. Cast off loosely, ribwise.

FINISHING OFF

Sew pocket onto outside of front over left side (as shown in illustration). Sew on button to correspond with buttonhole. Sew in sleeves, fitting each sleeve top into armhole shaping. Sew side and sleeve seams. Press seams according to instructions on ballband, do not press ribs.

FIVE-SQUARE JUMPER

**Needs some experience

SIZE
To fit bust 87-92(92-98,98-104)cm [34-36(36-38,38-40)in]

MATERIALS
Yarn used in sample
Jaeger Wool/Silk
Quantity
20(20,21) x 25g balls
Alternative yarn
Any other 4 ply yarn that knits up to same tension
Needles
1 pair each 3mm (11) and 3¼mm (10) needles
1 cable needle

TENSION
Using 3¼mm (10) needles over stocking stitch, 30sts x 40 rows = 10 x 10cm [4 x 4in] (see Tension, page 11).

Note Follow the basic set of instructions given for the Plain 4 Ply jumper (p127), but note that the increased sts worked in with the cable pattern are not included in the number of sts shown. Therefore, every time you have to count your sts, do not count in the extra ones; eg Row 1: K2 (inc in next st) twice, k2 – 6 sts have become 8 sts, but you only count them as 6 sts all the way through cable pattern. When casting off decrease the extra sts at the same time to keep number of sts and shape of jumper correct; eg casting off the example row above would be, cast off 2, k2tog twice, casting off as you go, cast off rem 2 sts.

BACK AND FRONT
Foll instructions for Plain 4 Ply jumper, but foll the chart sequence as shown and note special instructions above regarding extra sts increased over cable patt.
Foundation row (rs) P0(4,8); 6 sts cable patt (inc to 8); 37 sts from chart no 4; 6 sts cable patt; chart no 3; 6 sts cable patt; chart no 2; 6 sts cable patt; chart no 1 (plain st st); 6 sts cable patt; p0(4,8). (On ws rows k the p sts and p the k sts, ie reverse st st).
Now work charts on set sts working 4 rows of g st between each set of charts except for 6 st cable patt; keep this straight cable throughout work. Foll diagram for chart sequence.

SLEEVES
Foll instructions as given for Plain 4 Ply jumper but work in charts as folls:
Foundation row (rs) 6 sts cable patt (inc to 8); chart no 3; 6 sts cable patt; chart no 2; 6 sts cable patt. This row sets st and chart patt. Foll diagram for placing of chart patts, and work 4 rows of g st in between rows of charts as for back and front.

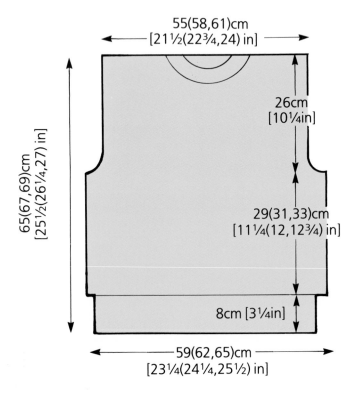

55(58,61)cm
[21½(22¾,24) in]

26cm [10¼in]

29(31,33)cm [11¼(12,12¾) in]

65(67,69)cm [25½(26¼,27) in]

8cm [3¼in]

59(62,65)cm [23¼(24¼,25½) in]

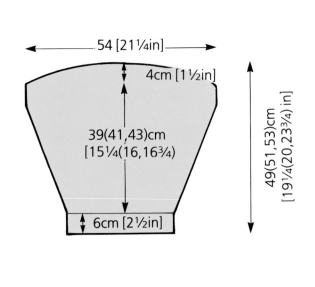

54 [21¼in]

4cm [1½in]

39(41,43)cm [15¼(16,16¾)

49(51,53)cm [19¼(20,23¾) in]

6cm [2½in]

CHART 1: 37 sts × 48 rows plain stocking stitch.

CHART 2

CHART 3

CHART 4

CHART 5

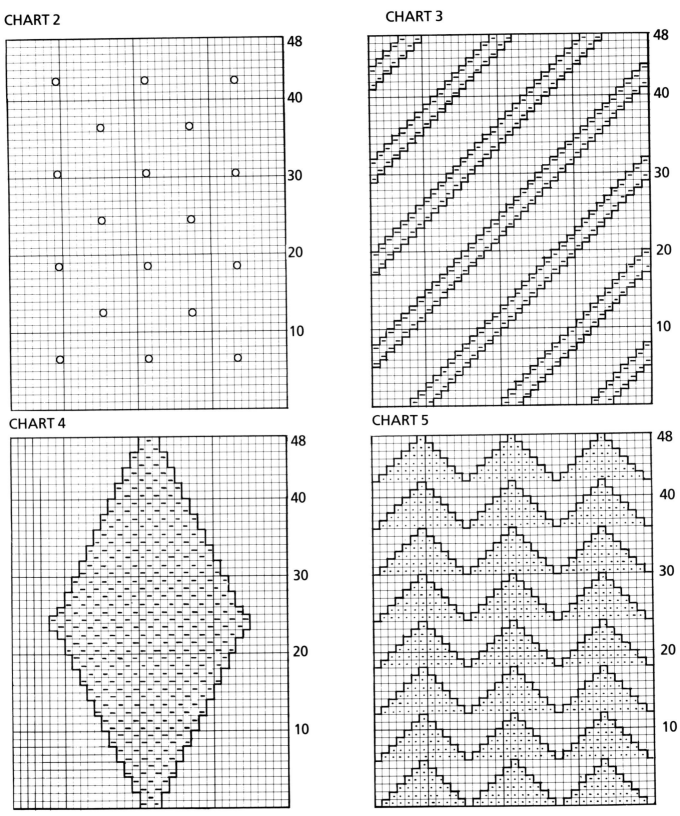

KEY

☐   RS rows – k: WS rows – p.

⊡   RS rows – p: WS rows – k.

   Reverse st st

   Moss stitch

O   Bobble – K, p, k in next st, turn, k3, turn, p3, turn, sl l, k2tog, psso.

◩   Inc in this st on first row only.

⬛⬜⬜   Cable – (Inc to 6 sts); Sl first 3 sts onto cable needle, hold at back, k3, k sts off cable needle.

Cable pattern – 6 sts inc to 8 in first row. Repeat these 8 rows throughout work.

CHART SEQUENCES
BACK AND FRONT

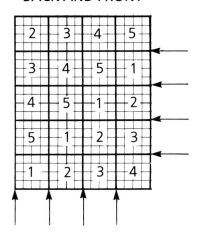

SLEEVES

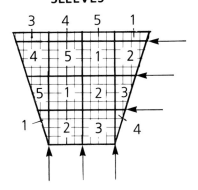

↑   Cable pattern between each chart.

←   Work 4 rows of G st between each row of charts.

4 PLY LINES

**Needs some experience

SIZE
To fit bust 87-92(92-98,98-104)cm
[34-36(36-38,38-40)in]

MATERIALS
Yarn used in sample
Jaeger Alpaca
Quantity
13(13,14) x 50g balls
Alternative yarn
Any other 4 ply that knits up to same
tension
Needles
1 pair each 3mm (11) and 3¼mm
(10) needles
1 cable needle

TENSION
Using 3¼mm (10) needles over
stocking stitch, 30sts x 40 rows =
10 x 10cm [4 x 4in] (see Tension,
page 11).

Note Follow the basic set of
instructions given for the Plain 4 Ply
jumper (p127), but note that the
increase sts worked in with the cable
pattern are not included in the
number of sts shown. Therefore,
every time you have to count your
sts, do not count in the extra ones; eg
Row 1: K2 (inc in next st) twice, k2 –
6 sts have become 8 sts, but you only
count them as 6 sts all the way
through cable pattern. When casting
off, decrease the extra sts at the same
time to keep number of sts and shape
of jumper correct; eg casting off the
example row above would be, cast off
2, k2tog twice, casting off as you go,
cast off rem 2 sts.

BACK AND FRONT
Foll instructions for Plain 4 Ply
jumper, but foll the chart sequence as
shown and note special instructions
above regarding extra sts increased
over cable patt.

Foundation row (rs) K9(13,17) sts
of chart no 1 (plain st st); 8 sts cable
patt (inc to 10); 31 sts of chart no 2; 8
sts cable patt twice (16 sts inc to 20);
50 sts chart no 3; cable patt twice; 31
sts chart 2; cable patt once; k9(13,17)
sts chart no 1 (plain st st).
This row sets the chart placings. Rep
the charts to end.

SLEEVES
Foll instructions as given for Plain 4
Ply jumper but work charts in
sequence as folls:
Foundation row Work last 5 sts of
chart no 2; 8 sts cable patt twice; 50
sts of chart no 3; cable patt twice;
first 5 sts of chart no 2.
Working on these sts as set, foll
shaping as given in instructions
bringing in rest of charts to match
back and front sequence as number
of sts allow.

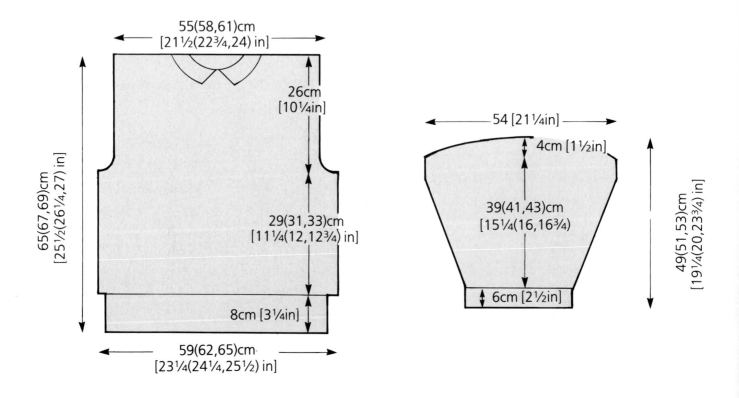

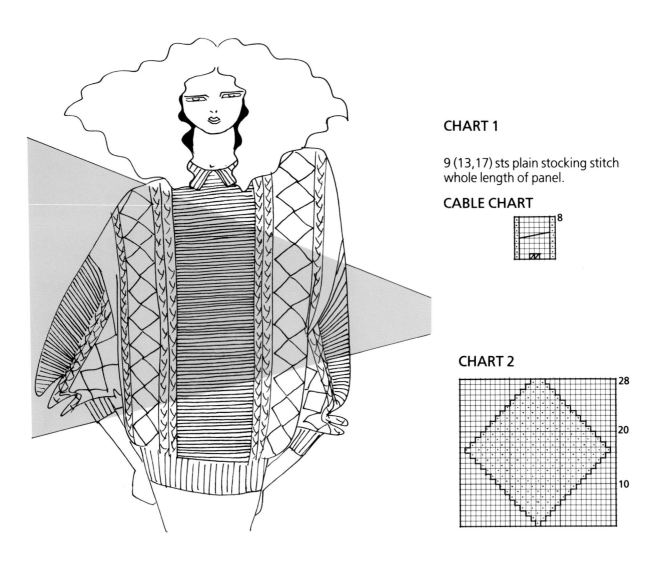

CHART 1

9 (13,17) sts plain stocking stitch whole length of panel.

CABLE CHART

8

CHART 2

28

20

10

CHART 3

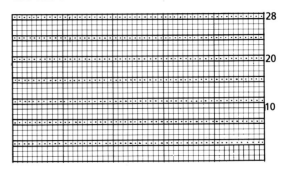

28

20

10

KEY

☐ RS rows – K; WS rows – P.

⊡ RS rows – P; WS rows – K.

⊞ Moss Stitch

⊠ Inc in this st on 1st row only.

▭▭▭ Cable (6 sts in to 8) – Slip first 4 sts onto cable needle, hold at back. K4, k sts off cable needle.

CHART SEQUENCE

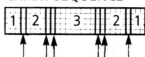

Cable pattern between each chart

MEN'S

CHUNKY CABLE

*Easy

SIZE
To fit chest 97-102(102-107,107-112)cm [38-40(40-42,42-44)in]

MATERIALS
Yarn used in sample
Kilcarra Cottage
Quantity
(Grey with black/oatmeal fleck 3617)
20(21,22) x 50g balls
Alternative yarn
Any chunky yarn that knits up to
same tension
Needles
1 pair each 5mm (6) and 6mm (4)
needles
1 cable needle

TENSION
Using 6mm (4) needles over stocking
stitch, 14sts x 22 rows = 10 x 10cm
[4 x 4in] (see Tension, page 11).

BACK
Rib With 5mm needles cast on
82(88,94) sts and work 6cm [2½in]
k2, p 2 rib. Change to 6mm needles
and work patt as folls:
Moss st patt
Row 1: K1, p1, k1, pl to end.
Row 2: P1, k1, p1, k1 to end. (Add
extra st when working over odd
number of sts.)
Cable patt
Foundation row: K3; (inc in next st)
twice; k3 (10 sts).
Row 2 and every alt row: P.
Rows 3,5,7,9,11: K.
Row 13: C10b (sl first 5 sts onto cable
needle and hold at back of work, k5, k
5 sts off cable needle).
Rows 15 & 17: K.
Row 18: P.
These 18 rows form cable patt repeat,
reading row 1 as row 3 for every
further repeat.
Sequence for back 22(24,26) sts

moss st; 8 sts cable patt (inc to 10
sts); 24 sts moss st; 8 sts cable patt
(inc to 10 sts); 22(24,26) sts moss st
[86(92,98) sts].
When work measures 40cm [15¾in]
from beg, shape for raglan.
Raglan shaping Row 1: Skpo, patt to
last 2 sts, k2tog.
Row 2: Keeping patt correct, patt
whole row**. Rep these 2 rows to
26(28,30) sts; leave sts on st holder/
spare yrn.

FRONT
As for back to **. Rep these 2 rows
until work measures 8cm [3¼in] less
than complete back. Keeping raglan
shaping correct, patt first 16 sts (15
when raglan worked), turn, work 1
row. Working on these sts only,
keeping raglan shaping correct, dec 1
st every alt row at neck edge to 1 st.
Fasten off. Leave centre 10(12,14) sts
on st holder and work rem sts to

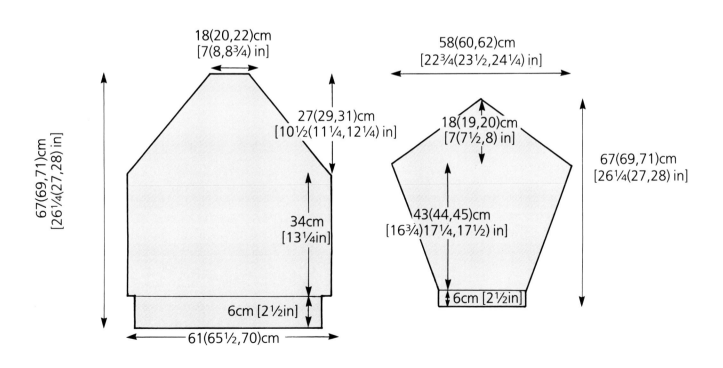

18(20,22)cm
[7(8,8¾) in]

58(60,62)cm
[22¾(23½,24¼) in]

27(29,31)cm
[10½(11¼,12¼) in]

18(19,20)cm
[7(7½,8) in]

67(69,71)cm
[26¼(27,28) in]

67(69,71)cm
[26¼(27,28) in]

34cm
[13¼in]

43(44,45)cm
[16¾)17¼,17½) in]

6cm [2½in]

6cm [2½in]

61(65½,70)cm

match left side, reversing shapings.

SLEEVES
Rib With 5mm needles, cast on 36 sts and work 6cm [2½in] k2, p2 rib, inc 4 sts evenly over last row [40 sts]. Change to 6mm needles and foll patt sequence thus:
Foundation row (rs) Work 16 sts moss st; 8 sts cable patt (inc to 10 sts); 16 sts moss st [42 sts]. At the same time inc 1 st each end of 5th and every foll 4th row until there are 82(84,86) sts, keeping extra sts as moss st. Work straight until sleeve measures 49(50,51)cm 19¼(19¾,20)in] from beg.
Raglan shaping Dec 1 st each end of every row to last 2 sts. Fasten off.

CREW NECK
Sew in left sleeve and front seam of right sleeve only. With rs facing, using 5mm needles, starting with back, puk 26(28,30) sts, 20 sts down side, 10(12,14) sts from front, 20 sts up side [76(80,84) sts]. Work 6cm [2½in] k2, p2 rib. Cast off loosely, ribwise. Sew in back seam of right sleeve and join neckband. Fold in half inwards and sew down inside.

FINISHING OFF
Sew side and sleeve seams.

TEXTURED CHUNKY

*Easy

SIZE

To fit chest 97-102(102-107,107-112)cm [38-40(40-42,42-44)in]

MATERIALS

Yarn used in sample

Kilcarra Cottage

Quantity

(Black with multicoloured fleck 4391) 20(21,22) x 50g balls

Alternative yarn

Any chunky yarn that knits up to same tension

Needles

1 pair each 5mm (6) and 6mm (4) needles

TENSION

Using 6mm (4) needles over stocking stitch, 14sts x 22 rows = 10 x 10cm [4 x 4in] (see Tension, page 11).

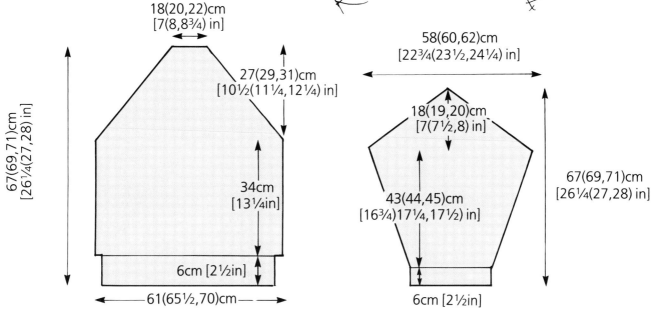

18(20,22)cm [7(8,8¾) in]

27(29,31)cm [10½(11¼,12¼) in]

67(69,71)cm [26¼(27,28) in]

34cm [13¼in]

6cm [2½in]

61(65½,70)cm

58(60,62)cm [22¾(23½,24¼) in]

18(19,20)cm [7(7½,8) in]

67(69,71)cm [26¼(27,28) in]

43(44,45)cm [16¾)17¼,17½) in]

6cm [2½in]

BACK

Rib With 5mm needles, cast on 80(86,92) sts and work 6cm [2½in] k2, p2 rib, inc 6 sts evenly over last row [86(92,98) sts]. Change to 6mm needles and foll patt thus:

Pattern 1 (6 sts x 12 rows)
Rows 1, 2 & 3: St st over 6 sts, starting with k row.
Row 4: K6. Rep these 4 rows twice more.

Pattern 2 (6 sts x 12 rows). Work 12 rows st st over 6 sts.

Pattern sequence
Rows 1-12: K1; *6 sts patt 1, 6 sts patt 2*; rep from * to * 7(7,8) times, rep 1st patt 0(1,0) more time; k1.
Rows 13-24: As 1 to 12 but work patt 2 followed by patt 1, to make squared effect.
When work measures 40cm [15¾in] from beg, shape raglan.

Raglan shaping
Row 1: SKPO, patt to last 2 sts, k2tog.
Row 2: Keeping patt correct, patt whole row**. Rep these 2 rows to 26(28,30) sts. Cast off.

FRONT

As for back to **. Work 8cm [3¼in] less than complete back. Keeping raglan shaping correct, patt first 16 sts (15 when raglan worked), turn, work 1 row. Working on these sts only, keeping raglan shaping correct, dec 1 st every alt row at neck edge to 1 st. Fasten off. Cast off centre 10(12,14) sts. Work rem sts to match left side, reversing shapings.

SLEEVES

Rib With 5mm needles cast on 38 sts and work 6cm [2½in] k2, p2 rib, inc 4 sts evenly over last row [42 sts]. Change to 6mm needles and work patt in the foll sequence: Start with (patt 1, patt 2) 3 times, patt 1, and work as given for back. At the same time inc 1 st each end of 5th and every foll 4th row to 82(84,86) sts. Work straight to 49(50,51)cm [19¼(19¾,20)in] from beg.
Raglan shaping Dec 1 st each end of every row to last 2 sts. Fasten off.

SHAWL COLLAR

With 5mm needles cast on 88(92,96) sts and work 4cm [1½in] k2, p2 rib. Change to 6mm needles and work further 6cm [2½in]. Cast off loosely ribwise. Sew in both sleeves. To sew in collar, pin cast-on edge of collar into neck opening, starting at beg of right-front shaping and ending at beg of left-front shaping, ie leaving centre cast-off edge free, and leaving short edges of collar free. Sew collar in place. Now sew left short edge of collar along cast-off edge of front, then right short edge of collar along cast-off edge of front, giving the 'shawl' effect. The collar will now fold over, if necessary sew a few securing sts at front to keep the collar lying down.

FINISHING OFF

Sew side and sleeve seams.

JUNKS

***Difficult

SIZE
To fit chest 97-102(102-107,107-112)cm [38-40(40-42,42-44)in]

MATERIALS
Yarn used in sample
Jaeger Matchmaker Twill
Quantities
Main colour (tarn 922) 7 x 50g balls (A)
1st contrast (logwood 923) 4 x 50g balls (B)
2nd contrast (roan 925) 3 x 50g balls (C)
3rd contrast (beech 926) 4 x 50g balls (D)
Alternative yarn
Any DK that knits up to same tension
Needles
1 pair each 3¼mm (10) and 4½mm (7) needles

TENSION
Using 4½mm (7) needles over stocking stitch, 22sts x 28 rows = 10 x 10cm [4 x 4in] (see Tension, page 11).

BACK
Rib With 3¼mm needles and A cast on 120(126,132) sts. Work k2, p2 rib for 10cm [4in].
Inc row Rib 4(7,10); (rib 3, inc in next st, rib 4) 14 times; rib 4(7,10) [134(140,146) sts]. Change to 4½mm needles and foll chart for back, working in st st and weaving yrn in on wrong side of work taking care not to pull work tight. Work to 64(66,68)cm [25¼(26,26¾)in] from beg.
Shoulder shaping Cast off 13(13,16) sts at beg of next 2 rows and 12(13,13) sts at beg of foll 6 rows. Cast off rem 36 sts.

FRONT
Work as for back until front measures 40(42,44)cm [15¾(16¼,17¼)in] from beg.
Neck shaping Patt 58(61,64) sts, turn and leave rem sts on spare needle. Keeping patt correct, dec 1 st at neck edge on every foll 4th row until 49(52,55) sts rem. Work straight to match length of back to shoulder shaping.
Shoulder shaping Cast off 13(13,16) sts at beg of next row and 12(13,13) sts at beg of foll 3 alt rows. Return to sts on spare needle. With rs facing, rejoin yrn and cast off first 18 sts; patt to end. Keeping patt correct, work to correspond with first side, reversing shapings.

SLEEVES
With 3¼mm needles and A, cast on 48 sts. Work k2 p2 rib for 6cm [2½in].
Inc row (Rib 1, inc in next st) 24 times [72 sts]. Change to 4½mm needles and foll chart for sleeve at the same time inc 1 st each end of 5th

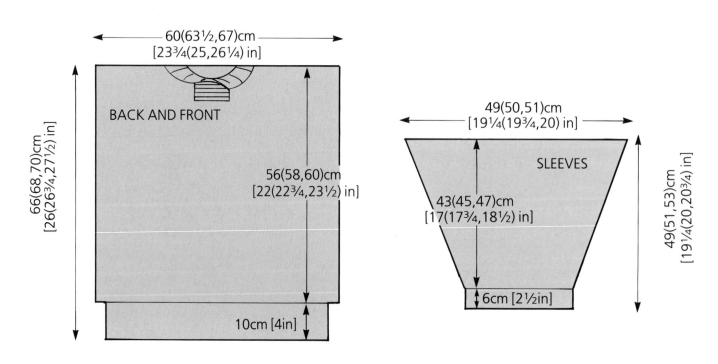

BACK AND FRONT

60(63½,67)cm [23¾(25,26¼) in]

66(68,70)cm [26(26¾,27½) in]

56(58,60)cm [22(22¾,23½) in]

10cm [4in]

SLEEVES

49(50,51)cm [19¼(19¾,20) in]

43(45,47)cm [17(17¾,18½) in]

49(51,53)cm [19¼(20,20¾) in]

6cm [2½in]

SLEEVES

and every foll 4th row until sleeve measures 49(51,53)cm [19¼(20,20¾)in] from beg. Cast off loosely.

COLLAR

With 3¼mm needles and A, cast on 190 sts and work k2, p2 rib for 4cm [1½in]. Change to 4½mm needles and cont in rib until collar measures 10cm [4in] from beg. Cast off loosely, ribwise.

FINISHING OFF

Press each piece separately (not collar) and do not press ribs. Join both shoulders using backstitch so that no cast-off sts are visible. Pin cast-on edge of collar into neck opening, starting at beg of right-front shaping and ending at beg of left-front shaping, leaving cast-off edge of front and two short ends of collar free. Sew collar neatly in place. Sew left short end of collar along cast-off edge of front, then right short edge of collar over left neatly. Sew in sleeves matching centre of each sleeve top with shoulder seam. Join side and sleeve seams. Press seams.

BACK AND FRONT

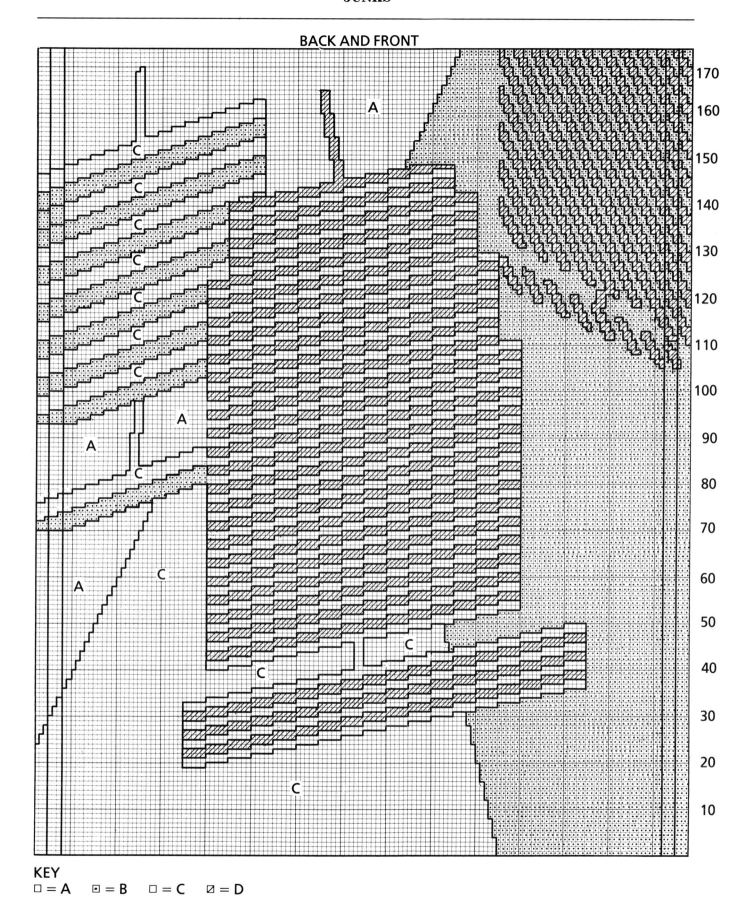

170
160
150
140
130
120
110
100
90
80
70
60
50
40
30
20
10

KEY

□ = A   ▣ = B   ▢ = C   ▨ = D

ACKNOWLEDGEMENTS

Many thanks to:

Steve Bannell for all his help and support.

Alison Margiotta for checking through the patterns.

Martin Palmer for his wonderful photography.

Andrea Hawkins for styling the jumpers beautifully and organising the models.

Yoshi for his marvellous way with hair and make-up.

Julia, Monica, Denise and Justin who modelled the jumpers, not forgetting Martin's dog Pippa – our live prop!

Pam Griffiths for making this book possible.

The knitters (in alphabetical order) – Mrs J. Bannell, Mrs C. Blackwell, Mrs J. Bowring, Mrs Brown, Mrs Canning, Mrs A. Castle, Mrs Cracknell, Mrs Durrant, Mrs Edwards and her team, Mrs P. Farley, Mrs Fields, Mrs D. Greener, Mrs Harris, Mrs Jarvis, Mrs Jones and her team, Mrs McAlister, Mrs Mather, Mrs T. Matthews, Mrs M. Mayfield, Mrs Mills, Mrs S. Nash, Mrs B. Richards, Mrs Snow, Mrs E. Stead, Mrs Thompson, Mrs O. Todd, Mrs Townsend and Mrs Watson.

YARN STOCKISTS

For your nearest stockist, please contact:

Jaeger Handknitting Ltd, PO Box Darlington, County Durham DL1 1YH; Tel (0325) 380123

Kilcarra, Groves of Thame Ltd, Lupton Road Industrial Estate, Thame, Oxon OX9 3RR; Tel (084 421) 3535

Rowan Yarns, Green Lane Mill, Washpit, Holmfirth, West Yorkshire; Tel (0484) 687714

Anne Rowena, 4 Trinity Street, Cambridge CB2 1SU; Tel (0223) 66841.
See also page 9 for information on knitting kits.

INDEX

CREDITS

Items of clothing worn in each photograph are as follows:

Spotlight Black pleated skirt by Emporio Armani; black woolly gloves with long cuffs by Cornelia James; black woolly tights by Aristoc Hosiery; Hiawatha black dexter loafers by the Natural Shoe Store.

Flower Trellis Black 501 jeans by Levi; Hiawatha black dexter loafers by the Natural Shoe Store; silver link earrings by Julie Bloom.

Roses Red chiffon and orange silk jacquard oblongs and red lambswool gloves with scalloped edges by Cornelia James; orange muslin crêpe long skirt by French Connection; pink blush opaque tights by Aristoc Hosiery; Hiawatha black dexter loafers by the Natural Shoe Store; gold and red ball drop earrings by Julie Bloom.

Flower Border Black wool lined leather gloves by Cornelia James.

Mohair Cable Black pleated skirt by Emporio Armani; black woolly tights by Aristoc Hosiery; Hiawatha black dexter loafers by the Natural Shoe Store; four-barred silver oval bracelet by Julie Bloom; silver beaded earrings to make yourself by the Bead Shop.

Mohair Jacket Blue 501 jeans by Levi; Hiawatha blue dexter loafers by the Natural Shoe Store.

Triangles Black riding breeches, boots, hat and gold topped crop by Kent Leather at Lillywhites.

Woolly Jumper Black wool lined leather gloves by Cornelia James; black riding breeches, hat, boots and gold topped crop by Kent Leather at Lillywhites.

Flower Squares Jeans shirt by Next for Men; red lambswool gloves with scalloped edges by Cornelia James; blue 501 jeans by Levi; gold and red ball drop earrings by Julie Bloom.

Raglan Mohair Black cotton embroidered skirt by Susan Bachouse; black 15 denier tights by Aristoc Hosiery; double row silver and turquoise necklace and gold and turquoise pumpkin earrings by Julie Bloom.

Long Mohair with Shirt Collar Black 501 jeans by Levi.

Bows White broderie anglaise '20s dress by Antiquarious; long string of pearls from a selection by Antiquarious; gold and light pink drop earrings by Julie Bloom.

Après Ski (Black & White) Black wool lined leather gloves by Cornelia James; black 501 jeans by Levi; four-barred silver oval bracelet and matching silver link earrings by Julie Bloom. (Turquoise, Pink & Citrus) Black woolly scarf and wool lined leather gloves by Cornelia James; black 501 jeans by Levi; black jodhpur boots by Kent Leather at Lillywhites; gold and deep pink drop earrings by Julie Bloom.

Abstraction Black woolly gloves with long cuffs by Cornelia James; black 501 jeans by Levi; black jodhpur boots by Kent Leather at Lillywhites.

Geo Pink muslin crêpe drop-waist skirt by French Connection; navy opaque tights by Aristoc Hosiery; gold and yellow ball drop earrings by Julie Bloom.

Paisley Black cloche hat by the Hat Shop; black pleated skirt by Emporio Armani; black 15 denier tights by Aristoc Hosiery; black commando-soled lace up shoes by the Natural Shoe Store; silver pear drop earrings by Julie Bloom.

Summer Border Black polo neck jumper by Marks & Spencer; red lambswool gloves with scalloped edges by Cornelia James; black cotton embroidered skirt by Susan Bachouse; red wool tights by Aristoc Hosiery; Hiawatha black dexter loafers by the Natural Shoe Store; turquoise and gold ethnic drop earrings by Julie Bloom.

All Over Paisley Natural 501 jeans by Levi; tan leather gloves by Chipie.

Festival Pink muslin crêpe short skirt by French Connection; navy opaque tights by Aristoc Hosiery; Hiawatha blue dexter loafers by the Natural Shoe Store; gold and yellow ball drop earrings and silver and blue bracelet by Julie Bloom.

Diamonds Vanilla straw hat by Laura Ashley; White broderie anglaise '20s dress by Antiquarious; vanilla opaque tights by Aristoc Hosiery.

Beauty Spot Black chiffon oblong by Cornelia James; black chiffon skirt with slip by Gamba Timeset; vanilla opaque tights by Aristoc Hosiery; gold triple bullit earrings by Julie Bloom.

Blooms Black men's hat by the Hat Shop; black woolly scarf and woolly gloves with long cuffs by Cornelia James; black 501 jeans by Levi; black jodhpur boots by Kent Leather at Lillywhites.

Aerobics Black woolly scarf and black woolly gloves with long cuffs by Cornelia James; black 501 jeans by Levi.

Flower Basket Taupe linen wide-legged trousers by Willi Wear; silver hoop earrings by Next the Jewellers.

Double Knitting Cable Cream straw hat with ribbons by Antiquarious; taupe wide-legged trousers by Willi Wear; tan leather gloves by Chipie; brown lace ups by Shelleys Shoes; silver filigree heart earrings by Next the Jewellers.

Garden Party '20s style cloche hat with antique bead clip by Antiquarious; taupe wide-legged trousers by Willi Wear; silver filigree heart earrings by Next the Jewellers.

Rose Jacket White Edwardian blouse by Antiquarious; long cream hobble skirt by Willi Wear; vanilla opaque tights by Aristoc Hosiery; tan Grenson lace ups by the Natural Shoe Store; silver filigree heart earrings by Next the Jewellers; silver filigree necklace by Antiquarious.

Flowering Delight Black woolly scarf by Cornelia James; long cream hobble skirt by Willi Wear; silver peardrop earrings by Julie Bloom.

Plain 4 ply Long brown wool skirt by Emporio Armani; brown opaque tights by Aristoc Hosiery; brown lace ups by Shelleys Shoes; silver bead earrings to make yourself by the Bead Shop.

Five Square Jumper Long cream hobble skirt by Willi Wear; long string of pearls from a selection at Antiquarious.

4 ply Lines Black cloche hat by the Hat Shop; black '20s chiffon dress with slip by Antiquarious; black 15 denier tights by Aristoc Hosiery; black suede moroccan slippers by Christine Ahrens; silver bead earrings to make yourself by the Bead Shop.

Chunky Cable Blue 501 jeans by Levi.

Textured Chunky Black 501 jeans by Levi.

Junks Navy chinos by Levi.

STOCKISTS

Antiquarious, Kings Road, London SW3
Bead Shop, The, Princes Street, London W1
Chipie, Floral Street, London WC2
Christine Ahrens, 11 Old Compton Street, London W1
Cornelia James, Harvey Nichols, Brompton Road, London SW3 and all major department stores
Emporio Armani, Sloane Street, London SW3
Gamba Timestep, St Martins Lane, London SW3
Hat Shop, The, Neal Street, London WC2
Julie Bloom, to order, telephone 01 731 6305
Lillywhites, 24-36 Regent Street, London W1 and branches
Natural Shoe Store, The, 21 Neal Street, London WC2; 325 Kings Road, London SW3; 22 Princes Square, Buchanan Street, Glasgow
Susan Bachouse, Hyper Hyper, Kensington High Street, London W8
Willi Wear, Neal Street, London WC2 and branches